The Art of
Body Talk

The Art of Body Talk

How to Decode Gestures, Mannerisms, and Other Non-Verbal Messages

GREGORY HARTLEY AND MARYANN KARINCH

CAREER
PRESS
Wayne, NJ

THE ART OF BODY TALK
Cover design by Howard Grossman/12E Design
Printed in the U.S.A.

The material in *The Art of Body Talk* has been previously published as *I Can Read You Like a Book*

To order this title, please call toll-free 1-800-CAREER-1 (NJ and Canada: 201-848-0310) to order using VISA or MasterCard, or for further information on books from Career Press.

The Career Press, Inc.
12 Parish Drive
Wayne, NJ 07470
www.careerpress.com

Library of Congress Cataloging-in-Publication Data

CIP Data Available Upon Request.

To Rick Hatten, a giant among men
—Greg Hartley

To Jim McCormick
—Maryann Karinch

Acknowledgments

First, thanks to Maryann for all these years of partnership and friendship. None of these books would have happened without the not-so-gentle insistence of our mutual friend, Michael Dobson—thank you. I can still remember the first conversation I ever had about body language with Doctor Larry Lewis all those years ago. Thanks, Doc. Thanks to Scott Rouse for helping me get back into the game in style. Thanks to the team at Career Press for being fantastic partners. Thanks to my family and friends, too numerous to mention, who have gotten me through some of the toughest years of my life. Thanks to Dina for being Dina.

—Greg Hartley

Thank you, Greg, for being such a great partner! You have enriched my knowledge of human behavior greatly and been such fun to work with these past dozen years. Thank you to Jim McCormick for keen insights, encouragement, and other practical support along the way. Great appreciation to Michael Dobson for introducing me to Greg. I am also grateful for the enthusiasm and support we have received from the Career Press team, specifically, Ron Fry, Michael Pye, Gina Schenck, Lauren Manoy, Laurie Kelly-Pye, and Karen Roy. We also very much appreciate the good work of Allison Olson, who has done an outstanding job of getting our work in print in many different languages. I also grateful for the fun with body language and promotion of our books that Gail Fallen makes possible on her KFKA show. Big thanks also to Shirley Sandler for spotting opportunities to tell the world about this book.

—Maryann Karinch

Contents

Introduction

Why You Need This Book

This book meets your need for practical information to help you get through a day, conflict with a friend, business challenges, sales pitches, and a heated election. In addition, it will also help you:

- Know the early warning signs of rage.
- Elect people who really know what they're talking about.
- Establish rapport quickly with customers.
- Contribute juicy insights to discussions about your favorite celebrities.
- Recognize love at first sight.
- Be the actor who nails every scene, and always gets the call back.

The book is a step-by-step guide to reading body language and using it to affect emotions, including your own and other people's.

Have you ever walked into a room and had someone greet you in a personal way, but you don't recognize her? Instantly, no matter how well your voice mimics familiarity, that individual knows you have no idea who she is. Not a great way to start a meeting, wedding reception, or a class reunion. If you knew a little about body language, you could easily convince her that you did recognize her.

If you knew a little more, you could put her at ease so quickly that she would tell you about herself, giving you distinct advantages in whatever conversation or negotiations ensued.

Turn the tables: She does not know who you are, but uses the fact that most people cannot admit memory lapse to get closer to you.

Most people who are good at reading body language can't tell you how they do it. They have not codified their instinctive ability, so the skills are not transferable. The edge we have over other body language experts is a combination of in-your-face (Greg) understanding why certain techniques work and replicating the effect, as well as research and extensive training of people in organizations who needed to upgrade their performance and weed out the losers and liars. It's a sense of causality between action and reaction.

You will not find our approach to the subject of body language, or even much of the vocabulary we use, in psychology textbooks. The concepts and words come from real life, not the lab.

Nevertheless, the approach we've refined through the years that builds on Greg's groundbreaking work with the R.E.A.D. system integrates new scientific knowledge and some re-shaped techniques. Some of them reflect behavioral changes we've catalogued because of entire generations growing up with technology that connects people instantly, regardless of their disparate cultures and where they are on the planet.

If you have this kind of methodical approach to reading body language, you can also develop the ability to use it in reverse. You can control your shadowy memory of body language to influence another person's behavior. It's possible to get what you want by manipulating body language and emotions together, both your own and the other person's. This is the crux of what interrogators do.

With skills in reading and using body language, you can daydream about other work you might do. Maybe you were not completely happy with the way a recent election turned out and you can now use your body language knowledge to help launch your new career as a politician. Maybe you'll grow up to be a negotiator in big business, for management or labor. Or maybe you'll get a more glamorous job, like a body language commentator for a news analysis show on television. Humans project what we are thinking, telegraphing the next move, and that allows people with body language knowledge to manipulate other people's train of thought.

When you get the skills, what are you going to do with them?

Part I:
Body Language Basics

1

The Steps to
Reading Body Language

Primitive man had a repertoire of survival skills that included reading body language. Etiquette and culture have blunted that natural human ability. Add to those factors the complexity of spoken language and modern conventions related to body language—stock gestures we see all the time in movies and television—and the result is: Few people today can read body language well.

Most of the time, we don't even know what our own bodies are doing. Human body language is more closely tied to ritual than planned behavior. We don't think about how to pick up a glass when we drink, how to hold a fork, or start a car. Our brains are so complex, with multiple subprograms running at all times, that it is difficult to have complete control over every twitch and tap. It is difficult for us to even remember what we've done if the action has reached the point of ritual or habit.

We teach professionals in finance and sales to read body language, as well as investigators and security professionals. For the latter groups, the survival of their careers, if not their lives, may depend on that ability.

In the following chapters, we will introduce you to a system Greg created called *R.E.A.D.*—Review, Evaluate, Analyze, Decide—which is an in-depth version of the course we teach government and business professionals in our body language classes. This is the same step-by-step training we give them, but we've added other modules, as well as a new system of reading moods, to make this book "the advanced course." These additional pieces address the interplay between body language and emotions, how to use gestures and posture as tools in business and personal relationships, and tricks to remain inscrutable by controlling how and when your own body language leaks emotions.

Take a minute and refer to the Contents. The next two paragraphs are a narrative complement to that outline, so you have a clearer understanding at the outset how the information in the book helps you build the skills of reading body language. In other words, if you skip around, you'll pick up some hot tricks, but you can't become adept at reading body language by taking that approach.

Beginning with some notes about communication of all beings, we move to distinctly human communication. The next topic figures prominently in our course on reading body language: culture. In this section, we look at the human groupings that have a profound impact on the way we express ourselves. You *cannot* hope to read body language well unless you take culture into consideration. Next, we move to person-to-person similarities, and then person-to-person differences. After that, you can start to answer the question: What are the differences between a person in a normal state—a state of congruence between gestures and voice—and a person in the state of sending verbal messages that conflict with non-verbal messages? At this point, the focus goes to the individual.

What is normal for a particular person? What is abnormal for a particular person? Those questions put us at the narrowest part of the diagram. From there, we start moving back toward a broader perspective. Exercises in applying the skill begin with a look at celebrities, who give us a common point of focus. You know the players; you see them every day on television. That sets the stage for reading the body language of individuals around you, for understanding their motivation and drive in context. As you practice overlaying the culture in your developing picture of what's happening, you can begin to employ the skill in one-on-one business and personal relationships, and then expanding the application of your expertise to groups.

Through time, your self-awareness of body language evolves as you review, evaluate, analyze, and decide what other people are doing. At that point, you've progressed to a level of knowledge and control that gives you powerful advantages over most other people.

What the Pros Know: TV Versus Reality

The ability of television cops and lawyers to catch a killer seems almost magical. For them, clues glow in the dark and fall out of the rafters. And when they interview a suspect, they read his body language to confirm his guilt. Given the advantage of close-ups, and a director explaining when and how to mimic a behavior, you get to see what tips off the brilliant detective—but you don't necessarily know what it means. Rubbing the legs while he's talking (stress relief through energy displacement), pupils opening like windows to take in more information when he sees a photo of the victim, and dry mouth (another sign of intense anger), all fit together for the smart cop, but all you perceive is a feeling that the suspect is an emotional wreck. These actors are, of course, working from a script, so they know the subtext, which the writer may or may not have gotten right. The truth is often much more subtle and difficult to read. Human subroutines can become really complex, and it is a rare combination of talent and experience that enables the writer-director-actor team to get it right. Greg has partnered with writer and producer Christopher Pratt to develop this dance in some of Pratt's work.

Homeland is a provocative show from a body language perspective because Carrie Mathison (Claire Danes) moves between keen analysis and warping the meaning of what she observes. In the earlier seasons, the CIA operations officer goes to great lengths to prove that every move U.S. Marine Sergeant Nicholas Brody makes when he returns home after eight years in captivity in Iraq signals his readiness to betray America. She firmly believes that Al-Qaeda turned Brody while he was their prisoner—and her conviction creates a filter that distorts some of what she sees him doing.

Mathison plants cameras in nearly all of the rooms of Brody's suburban Washington, D.C., house and watches him do everything from pour wine to have sexual relations with his wife. In the time the surveillance cameras are there, she sees things that give her clues as to who he is and what his true emotions and intentions are, and at the same time, she sees what she wants to see in his actions.

Just a day after his arrival back in the States, she participates in debrief at CIA headquarters. A trained interrogator, she calls him out on a statement that he made earlier to military debriefers that he didn't divulge any strategic or tactical information to his captors. "My SERE training was excellent," he replies. Pressing him further, Mathison asks why he would have been kept alive for eight years if he told them nothing. Brody remains relatively unflappable, at first only giving a crooked smile to suggest that he isn't telling the small CIA group everything. But as she pushes on, asking if Brody recognizes a significant Al-Qaeda terrorist in a photo she hands him, we see an eye twitch when he denies knowing him. Mathison sees the twitch, too. Brody denies knowing the Al-Qaeda leader: "No, I never met him." But the television audience knows—and Mathison knows—that he's lying. She sees signs of a false denial, including penetrating, sustained eye contact from Brody.

Later, with her suspicions raging, Mathison speculates that Brody is sending signals with subtle hand movements that are visible during his media interviews. However, nearly everyone else at the CIA is ready to dismiss them as nervous gestures.

Is she reading him well or projecting meaning onto the movements? To complicate matters, she finds Brody attractive—different filter, different kind of distortion.

Greg taught at SERE, the acronym for Survival, Evasion, Resistance, and Escape, a program that provides U.S. military personnel and other selected people in the military with training in evading capture, survival skills, and the military code of conduct. Many of the military people who go through SERE have a very high risk of capture. We know for sure that Sergeant Brody's training would have been excellent. In fact, it may have been so excellent that Brody's self-control is believable. And yet, he leaked clues of deception that a trained eye could see.

Greg's body language students were aspiring interrogators and human intelligence collectors in both military and non-military sectors of government service and they were hand-picked for his body language class. They come through the door embracing a paradox of their own creation: "I'm good enough to be in this class so I must already know most of what Hartley's going to teach me."

They often referenced John Travolta's 2003 movie *Basic*, which "taught" them that a person looking up and to his right means he's lying; Greg told them that they've been deceived. A broad conclusion such as this about a particular piece of body language usually has very little meaning. Until they are connected with other factors, and until you have baselined a person to determine what is normal behavior, you can't draw a conclusion about truth or deception based on a single eye movement. If you want to "read someone like a book," you need to look at the entire text and not just the section titles.

Another common misconception is that crossed arms always signify a barrier, a defensive gesture to block someone out, primarily because of insecurity. This gesture alone means nothing. Stand in front of a mirror. Cross your arms, furrow your brow, point toward the mirror with your head, and overly enunciate the words, "Do I seem insecure?" The answer: No, you don't.

Some of the other mistaken beliefs even come from "expert" sources writing about human patterns of behavior. They see a phrase such as "Seventy-three percent of the time, a man with his fingers in a steepling position is feeling self-confident" and conclude that the theory applies to all steepling—up, down, or sideways. Not so, as you will soon find out.

Using numbers like this to justify a conclusion about human behavior borders on nonsense. Assigning numbers to behavior patterns is an attempt to mask uncertainty. Humans are easily represented on a bell curve for any demographic. The greatest percentage is going to fall somewhere near the center with extreme deviations lying near the edges. This works for intelligence, skin tone, how white your teeth are, and how many times you have skinned your knee. It is not magic; it is simple math.

Even after the intelligence students go through the basic body language course, they often allow their projections to contaminate what they observe, just as Carrie Mathison does with Brody. The turning point tends to be their failure to successfully pinpoint the bad guy in a scenario that serves as a kind of final exam.

Let's consider one of those scenarios. If you determine what kind of body language the terrorist would have, then you are on the road to expertise in this field.

The Scenario

The scene is a farmhouse in northern Iraq in 2007. You and two people in your unit have been briefed that an informant alleges that someone in that house is an IED (improvised explosive device) kingpin. You have room for only one person in your transport, so you must find the individual that is most likely to be that person. In addition, you know that this person is known as Abulhul, or "father of despair." That's what the Sphinx is called in Egyptian, by the way.

You and your buddies kick the door in and find five people in the room having dinner—a middle-aged Iraqi male and two Iraqi couples. Everyone in the house appears to be Iraqi because of their physical appearance and clothing; everyone speaks an Iraqi dialect. At this point, you have one hour to determine who the terrorist is and get that person back to your unit.

You ask one of the men, who has a noticeable scar across his forehead: "What do you do for a living?"

"I sell timers and radios," he replies. He wrings his hands and rubs his head. Have you struck gold immediately?

His cousin, one of the other men in the room, admits to being an electronics repairman. "Don't listen to that stupid man," he says. He explains that his cousin suffered a serious head injury and functions only on a marginal level. He has trouble remembering words; instead of saying clocks, he said timers. "I try to help him," the man says, "by giving him clocks and radios that I repair to sell."

Suspicion now moves to the electronics repairman. You keep an eye on him, as he taps his fingers on the table and shifts in his chair. He clearly resents your presence, but says nothing.

You watch him out of the corner of your eye as you question his wife. She appears to be a simple woman who gives straightforward answers to questions, but clearly hates Americans. With nowhere to go during the day, she sits home and watches television with her kids around the clock. The farmhouse is equipped with satellite TV, so she not only gets news, but also American crime shows, and a plethora of programs that cause her to conclude that the United States has a population of immoral, insane people. She spits at you and the other soldiers as her husband gestures for her to sit down and shut up.

The electronics repairman's brother owns the house; he's a sheep farmer who makes a point that he has a thriving business. He uses his arms to indicate that his flock is enormous and that they keep him busy night and day. His wife has two kids at home and, similar to her sister-in-law, all she does is take care of the kids all day. From the way she answers questions, she seems to be more educated than the other woman.

After you ask a barrage of standard questions, such as "Where you were born?" and "How long have you lived here?" the tactic you and your buddies use is to ask questions designed to make each person leak information about the others. You go after the woman who is vocal in her anti-Americanism and suggest she's obviously alone in her feeling.

"No!" she screams and points again and again to her sister-in-law. "Ask her. She knows what they're like!"

The other woman strides from where she was standing and faces you directly. "Yes, I know because I saw for myself how you kill," she says quietly. "She sees it only on TV."

The Answer Revealed

The students who figure out who the guilty party generally do so through questioning and by putting aside their preconceived notions that the "father of despair" must be a man. Good questioning of the woman who hates Americans will reveal that she does not like or trust her sister-in-law, whom she does not consider a real Iraqi. Why? The wife of the shepherd left Iraq when she was 10 years old because her father was on the outs with the Saddam regime. Her family lived in Germany until after the first Gulf War, and then came back, thinking that the Shi'ites would take power.

A star student of body language will notice three telling things: First, the wife of the electronics repairman points at the other woman in an accusing way as she says, "Ask her!" Second, the other woman moves in a way that suggests she has only recently started wearing Iraqi garb again. A woman who had worn pants for a period of time would stride, but not a woman who has worn a dress and lived among traditional Iraqi women her whole life. Third, the shepherd's wife approached her questioner directly, which is uncharacteristic behavior. She has a Western woman's sense of comfort talking face-to-face with a man.

The truth you need is this: She still has friends in Germany and mules sensitive information back and forth. She is the source of sophisticated design information and supplies for new IEDs.

The moral of the story is this: Don't jump to conclusions based on things you think are true. Watch and listen for clues that add up logically, not ones that fit a pattern you think should be there.

One of the photos we've shown to provoke analysis in various body language workshops invariably gets the same reaction. The photo captures the face of a white-haired old woman, smiling slightly, and wearing a simple checkered housedress. The students uniformly respond with descriptors, such as "weak," "frail," and "helpless." It's the photo of a 96-year-old Florida woman who gunned down her nephew with a .357 magnum handgun in 2011. This assumption of zero-threat from an elderly person is rooted in a cultural bias. In a culture that values youth and vigor, the old cannot possibly be dangerous. Most Americans never consider what they would think if they met a 74-year-old Harrison Ford who didn't have the benefit of makeup and a good camera angle. Is he still Indiana Jones, or is he suddenly Professor Henry Jones?

Sheikh Omar Abdel-Rahman, who is now serving a life sentence at the Butner Federal Correctional Institution in Butner, North Carolina, is a blind Muslim cleric. Linked to the 1993 World Trade Center bombing, among other heinous acts, he may have looked pathetic, but his fatwa calling for violence against U.S. civilian targets made a powerful terrorist.

What We Teach the Pros

Communication

We can break human communication into three channels:

1. **Verbal:** Word choice.
2. **Vocal:** All human voice components that do not include word choice.
3. **Non-verbal:** All other pieces of communication.

Think of verbal communication as the servant of the will: It is the easiest channel to control. People can more easily select their words than they can control their nervous coughs or eye tics. Think about how much more powerful your communication becomes as you increase your level of control over the other two as well.

The vocal aspect of communication is a kind of packaging: It gives a "look and feel" to the verbal expression. There's no doubt that you've had exposure to someone so well-spoken that simply hearing him or her inspires you. When Greg was a young soldier, he worked for a lieutenant with this gift—a thoroughly impressive man until Greg realized the lieutenant was speaking at half the speed of everyone else. That gave him time to choose each word carefully. Great speakers not only make precise word choices, but they control cadence, similar to the lieutenant, as well as tone, pitch, and a host of utterances that are part of the vocal component of communication.

The third channel—non-verbal—includes gesturing, posture, proximity to others, and other factors explored throughout this book. A premise of the approach we teach is that, in terms of non-verbal communication, there are fewer differences than similarities among people, otherwise we couldn't communicate as a species.

Merriam-Webster defines "communication" as "A process by which information is exchanged between individuals through a common system of symbols, signs, or behavior." Although your brain may focus on the last part of the definition—symbols, signs, or behavior—focus on a couple of words that precede it, namely, *process* and *system*. "Process" is what occurs between the beginning and the end. It implies causality. "System" describes independent parts coming together into an organized whole. For example, rage may be sparked by a thought, but the communication of it is the process that includes a balled fist, an arm that goes rigid, contracting pupils, a stiff back, and so on.

The end point may be the enraged person planting his knuckles on some other guy's jaw. This rage can be communicated without intent, too, as long as you know the sequence of body movements that effectively convey it. A good interrogator has the capacity to communicate rage where there is none, just as a good actor does. Although many interrogators believe that this is the most difficult emotion to portray, it isn't. Few people have ever seen true rage.

Therefore, given that communication means a bit more than a single grunt or foot stomp, a typical first question from students is "Do animals communicate?"

The simple answer is "Yes." Cats, dogs, horses, goldfish, hamsters, and monkeys all have a system of symbols and behavior that convey information. But let's draw a distinction here between those actions that take shape as communication and simple, non-verbal behavior. When a cat scratches her ear, she isn't trying to tell you anything; she's scratching because her ear itches. Keep this distinction in mind for human behavior, too. Sometimes a scratch is just that.

The difference between animal communication and human communication is, of course, complexity. Our pets generally communicate in a series of utterances, shifts in posture, flexing of extremities, and eye movement. The most mentally advanced of these animals, the primate, has monkeys on the low end of the spectrum and great apes toward high end. Beyond them, sitting at the tip of this communication chain, is the greatest of apes: human beings. Think of man as the shaved ape, which is a take-off on Desmond Morris's *The Naked Ape*. We are not "naked," as much as "shaved," meaning that we try very hard to remove the animal from who we are.

Ironically, one of the things we've done in becoming a sophisticated species, anointing ourselves as the rulers of the planet, is add nuances and complexity to our communication that often makes it more—not less—difficult to communicate precisely with each other. Many animals communicate complex ideas, but they do it using utterances that have unambiguous meanings.

For example, vervet monkeys give specific alarm calls that indicate which type of predator is in the neighborhood. These monkeys that live in the rainforests of Africa verbally communicate the exact nature of a threat to their tribe.

To signal that an eagle has been spotted, a vervet will make a low-pitched grunt. When a leopard is spotted, however, the vervet sings a series of distinct tones. Lastly, when a python is spotted, a vervet will give a high-pitched staccato barking sound, called a "chutter."

These are the three main predators of the vervets, so it makes sense that vervets would call out when they spot one of these animals. However, having different calls for each predator is really powerful because these three predators all hunt very differently and thus a different escape strategy is necessary for each one.[1]

A very effective system of symbols would be one that conveyed our thoughts as precisely as the vervets do in this example. Even with the most astute communicators, spoken English can be confusing. For example:

No reading aloud.

No reading allowed.

Homonyms, multiple meaning of words and connotations that overtake the denotations of words (for example, *terrific*) all make English a tough language to learn. The French Academy makes rules to avert this kind of mess; we in the United States seem to enjoy the creative exercise of fostering the mess.

Now read this aloud: Would you prefer to lie?

What is the meaning? It could be an accusation, or asking about a choice of relaxation. Whether in print or spoken, you cannot tell. Should you be insulted if a person says this to you? Maybe you look tired and don't know it. How much of the meaning comes through in the spoken words? How much of the meaning would the speaker convey through body language? Would a slight drop of the brow or scowl of the lips help you to understand? How about tone and inflection? Emphasis on *you* carries a different sense from an emphasis on *prefer*. How much do you think an accent or pronunciation would impact comprehension of the meaning if you simply heard the sentence on the radio?

Akin to our chimp cousins, we convey information on many channels, and although we prefer to think of ourselves as so much more, we respond to these signals as readily as our chimp cousins. It means that someone who better understands the cues and meanings can control the conversation in a way even Machiavelli himself, with his humanist beliefs, could not imagine.

By missing the animal piece of communication—shrieks, limbs flailing, eyes darting, and arched back—we reduce our ability to comprehend. No language alone can reach the subtlety of spoken language overlaid on effective non-verbal communication.

Body Movement

We all understand body language on *some* level; most people simply do not pay attention to the subtle pieces of daily communication. Many people can see body language on a subconscious level, but they override their perceptions. We are taught to "be logical," as if there were such a thing as logic when dealing with most humans.

Reading vocal and non-verbal communication is the real meat of the subject—the "voodoo," or reading the unintentional cues presented by the source. In other words, what is the other person telling me that he really does not want me to know?

After moving through the body-language curriculum, the next stage is learning the offensive applications, or how to influence someone gently into what you want. You can think of this as "interrogator mind tricks," an obvious reference to George Lucas's inflated version of this, the Jedi mind tricks. The connection is intimate: Tap in on a subconscious level to a person's mind to get the response you want or need.

The systematic process begins with baselining, and then moves to review of individual body parts.

Baselining

Baselining is a portable version of the polygraph. You use it to pick up subtle variables in body language and tone of voice. Once you know what to look and listen for, you can detect changes that accompany stress of varying degrees. That ability gives you a high degree of control in your interaction with someone.

Starting with the mid-section of the book, we emphasize the importance of observing the body language of an individual in a relaxed state; that is, seeing what happens naturally, without affectation or stress. We highlight what gestures and physical responses are involuntary and universal, because these are *not* what you focus on in baselining. You will take every other kind of signal and physical response into consideration, however.

Body Parts

In beginning the scan of body movements, let's start with the face. To steal the words of Desmond Morris, the face is the organ of expression. Our agreement ends there. Morris conjectured that it is the easiest to control because it is the closest to the brain, but we disagree. When it comes to the face, we're dealing with a paradox: The face is both the easiest and the hardest area of the body to control. There are many things we do with our faces that we aren't even aware of. They are second nature.

A lot of emotion comes out through the brow in both voluntary and involuntary expressions. We use the forehead muscles when we normally interact with people, even on the phone, and we develop wrinkles as a result. If Morris was right and we can control the muscles in the face more easily than others, then we wouldn't be using so much Botox. We could voluntarily stop using the muscles that create the problem, and even voluntarily reverse the process of wrinkling by exercising them. In addition, if the face were under our control, more facial movements would be cultural, not universal.

Facial movements become practiced behavior over time, because we learn how to present an even smile when meeting someone and an arched eyebrow when our kid drops mustard on the floor. But the plethora of muscles in our face makes it hard for us to keep track of them. We often do not even realize the range of emotions and physiological reactions we express with our faces. What does that upturned brow mean? Is there a difference if the person sending the message is male or female? If the receiver is male or female? How do the sexes differ in messaging, not only with the same sex but the opposite sex? Is that well-intended signal misread because of differences in the two brains? The head is the workhorse of communication. And although much of what it conveys is intentional, we still leak messages that are impossible to cover.

From the head, face, and neck, we move to the arms, down to through the rest of the body: hands and gesturing, torso, legs, and feet. Do those folded arms really mean the person is guarded and maybe even disgusted? Do those crossed feet indicate you are shutting me out? This is where people's absolutes start to break down, because they learn that you can't draw conclusions without understanding context.

Context

An involuntary movement cannot be understood out of context. In other words, John Travolta can't figure out if a guy is lying simply by looking at his pupil movement. The pupils enlarge to take in more information and contract to block it out, but unless you have a knowledge of context, you don't have the information you need to evaluate the meaning. That action does give you a clue about the person's emotional state, but without context you will not know if the pupils dilated because of sexual arousal or fear, or if they narrowed to pinpoints because of disgust.

The stage an actor is on affects the message and that is also the case with all human communication. A person's surroundings can affect the message he is sending as well as how you receive it. Context contains a number of elements in addition to gestures and facial expressions, such as space, time, and even smell.

You

Finally, we will ask you to use your lifelong learning to help discern what all that signaling means. We can teach you some new tools, but years of specialized knowledge will make you a unique body language communicator—a little different from anyone else in the world.

What to Expect

At the end of this program on reading body language, you will look at everyone differently. From coworkers or employees to in-laws, you will have a more intelligent understanding of what the other chimps are saying to you.

They, and now you, will look at newsreels of Adolf Hitler's wild, flailing arms and see something that his desperate followers did not. You will understand why, years after his insane despotry, many people still call him a communications genius; you will perceive the mechanisms that allowed him to be effective. You will also see gestures that bleed sickness.

You will regain something your primitive ancestors used daily: a second sight to body language.

2

Culture:
The Big External Influence

All animals have a culture and a language associated with that culture. Whether the language contains words or some other vocalization, all of these cultures will include body language. For example, horses are limited in vocabulary to a series of soft snickerings, shrill screeches, and plaintive wails. Their body language further enhances communication style, although it's limited because they need all four limbs to stand upright. They adapt by using eye movement, sudden action, raising a hoof, pinning ears, and threats of physical action to communicate their messages. All horses therefore have the capacity to "speak" to each other with common "language" that is ubiquitous within their species.

Interestingly, even though horses have the same "vocabulary," they use it with different inflections. If you take a horse from one herd and drop her into a new herd, something strange occurs: The new horse may try to communicate with the softer or the harsher body language and communication style it is accustomed to. She tries to fit in with the new crowd in a way that worked for her in the previous group, which often leads to an unfortunate outcome. The new gang reacts violently, sometimes because the horse is new, but other times because the alpha doesn't like certain kinds of behavior. For instance, the new gelding tries to buddy up to the old gelding on the side of the herd by offering some friendly scratching, but the old gelding sees that as a threatening move due to herd dynamics. In effect, this horse herd has created variances in its body language that are specific to its culture.

Now let's take it a step further. Most of us in the species are capable of the same actions as others in our species. We don't have control over our ears to pin them and send a harsh message, nor do we have access to the hooves to strike out quickly. We do, however, have sudden movement, we can roll our eyes and tense our muscles, and we can inject shrillness into our voice. We also have a huge retinue of movements and adapted signals to use that most humans can understand without education.

Imagine leaving a bunch of toddlers to their own devices to develop a language. What would happen? One individual would likely establish dominance over time because we are herd animals, but in the beginning, each of them would speak his or her own brand of gibberish, and try to get the other one to understand. All of the toddlers would get frustrated, and with no rules some would rely on biting or hitting, while some would try more civil means to communicate.

The sharpest of the little band would notice when some of her hand-waving and body movement got the results she wanted and would do it over and over. As her results increased, others would adapt this same signaling and start using the tools of the superior communicator. The toddler effectively created a gesture to communicate and this communication would eventually be understood by her whole band. When a new toddler later became part of the group, the new one would need to understand the meaning of that particular body language. It wouldn't matter what the new toddler wanted the meaning to be since the meaning was set by the pre-existing culture of toddlers.

Assuming no physical anomalies, all humans are born capable of making the same movements. With no common language, we can assign meaning to any movement made. When meaning has been assigned to a movement it takes away the individual's ability to create meaning or use the body in that given way to mean anything other than the universally agreed context. *For this reason, culture curtails human body language.* It cannot add to anything we are born with. All it can do is limit meaning and assign ubiquitous meaning to an action.

For example, consider "hand talk" of Native Americans, more formally referred to as Plains Indian Sign Language (PISL), or Plains Sign Talk, as it's called in Canada. By using the hands and four basic factors—location of hand, movement, shape, and orientation—people from 37 oral languages reaching across 12 language families in an area of 1 million square miles of the North American continent could effectively communicate.[1] That meant the people who arrived from Spain with their own brand of signaling had a far less sophisticated and less formalized unspoken language than the Native Americans they encountered. Only through trial and error, and certainly many false messages, did these groups learn to communicate.

Ruthless Celtic kings and their chiefs had body language that both defined and separated them as well. A nasty, belching bunch, they could easily be identified by "hands twitching to the sword hilt at the imagined hint of an insult...wiping the greasy moustaches that were a mark of nobility," in the words of anthropologist Stuart Piggott in *Ancient Europe*.[2]

From Sub-Culture to Super-Culture

Whether we're talking about Native Americans, Spanish invaders, or Celtic warriors, every human culture has the same binding elements: beliefs, traditions, behaviors, and rules. These elements work together to engender security within the group and keep people riding in the same direction. Culture separates one group from another, enabling them to know who to tolerate and who to view with suspicion.

Culture is nothing more than accepted social norms for a group. They can develop by consensus or through a follow-the-leader process. With that in mind, consider that cultures can arise from small subgroups, or micro-cultures, all the way up to humankind. In terms of our study of body language, the concept of micro-cultures includes couples: male-female, female-female, or male-male. Every pairing or grouping has created norms for what is acceptable. More importantly, every micro-culture has created taboos as well. Cultures that reach across humankind become what we call a super-culture. With modern media saturation and global product marketing, gestures, words, and even attitudes can become super-cultural.

For a long time, many language experts maintained that *okay* and *Coca-Cola* were the most recognized words in the world. With the proliferation of web access, we share a much larger and diversified vocabulary of expressions, product names, and even insults. Words like *drone* and *meme* are used heavily around the world. And many more brands than Coca-Cola, as well as proper names like Steve Jobs and Pope Francis, have joined the ranks of words recognized worldwide, regardless of the language. Maryann works with an associate in Bangladesh on web projects and if she says "404," she doesn't have to explain that it's code for an online error. The linguistic shift contributes to the growing super-cultural nature of online communication.

Certain behavioral changes have occurred almost universally as well. With the widespread adoption of mobile, personal technologies, we could argue that changes in behavior, and changes in culture, are Lamarckian as opposed to Darwinian. Jean-Baptiste Lamarck was a naturalist and contemporary of Charles Darwin's, with the two of them having different perspectives on evolution. Lamarck focused on evolutionary change that occurs within the lifespan of a single organism rather than taking multiple generations to occur completely. It's the principle of "change through use or disuse," like a giraffe permanently lengthening its neck to reach the only edible leaves in its environment.

Neuroscientist Vilayanur Ramachandran has a theory on how this potentially occurs with behavior and culture. Ramachandran, director of the Center for Brain and Cognition and distinguished professor with the psychology department and neurosciences program at the University of California, relies a great deal on the work of Giacomo Rizzolatti and his team at the University of Parma regarding mirror neurons.

In 2005, Rizzolatti published a paper titled "Observing Others: Multiple Action Representation in the Frontal Lobe"[3] and followed that in 2008 with a book called *Mirrors In The Brain: How Our Minds Share Actions and Emotions.* There are around 100 billion neurons in the adult human brain; subsets of these, called mirror neurons, are located in the front of the brain. They fire when a person performs a specific action; however, Rizzolatti discovered that they also fire when people watch other people doing something. Ramachandran compares it to a virtual reality simulation of the other person's action. He therefore posits that the significance of the mirror neurons is that they are involved in imitation and emulation: "Because to imitate a complex act requires my brain to adopt the other person's point of view."[4]

Ramachandran then goes out on a scientific limb, but he makes a lot of sense. He speculates that the great leap forward in human evolution that occurred roughly 50,000 years ago may be attributable to the sudden emergence of a sophisticated mirror neuron system. If he is correct, then when one Homo erectus discovered that rubbing two rocks together produced a spark, it set in motion the adoption of the same fire-making process very rapidly: "Instead of dying out, this spread rapidly, horizontally across the population, or was transmitted vertically, down the generations. So, this made evolution suddenly Lamarckian, instead of Darwinian."[5]

Consider that all of these changes occurred within a single generation: typing with thumbs, normalizing body art, self-documenting life events, and conveying intimate information through hand-held devices. They are memes, that is, elements of culture that occur through imitation, rather than genetic changes. They force us to rethink the meaning of another person's physical, verbal, and vocal communication. They are signs that a culture is changing; they are the harbingers of a new "normal." As society becomes more interconnected, the amalgamation of ideas runs much more rapidly. An idea that would have once taken a generation can now become normalized in days if not months.

In past generations a person's voice was limited to the influence he created through some channel, most often formal, but occasionally informal. This kind of influence often had gate keepers to stymie the would-be great orator and stop him from achieving a platform to spread ideas. A given idea would have to bypass the "establishment," or guards, of the organization he was trying to change.

MySpace was one of the social media efforts that started to change that, but it was Facebook that transformed the communications landscape. Founded in 2004, in just 12 years, Facebook went from being a Harvard-only social networking service to a company with 1.23 billion monthly active users worldwide and a market valuation of $350 billion.

On the positive side Facebook creates a platform for societies to interact and normalize communication styles. The more exposure we have to each other, the more the mirror neurons fire, helping to create shared experiences and ideas; organisms morph to think and react as one society instead of many. You can find pockets of this happening all over the world as result of Facebook. Wherever free communication is tolerated, ideas can move at the speed of electricity—and effect cultural shifts just as rapidly. We still have newspapers, but not their censorship and control of ideas.

The emergence of Facebook allows a person to have a voice. This voice affects our propensity to relate and imitate as well. Insidiously, and unlike the celebrated Abraham Lincoln standing on a stump in the town square and addressing bystanders, the Facebook world allows people to gather like-minded folks at the outset and deliver a message that is sure to resonate. This resonating drives ideas and mental change to move rapidly through a population—unchecked. It is like a virus dropped into a non-resistant host and left to replicate until it becomes overwhelming, and then it emerges in the greater population. This virus has an advantage no other does: It can eliminate anything that disagrees or opposes it with the click of an "unfriend" button. This is by no means limited to Facebook. Look at the widespread growth of ISIS (Islamic State of Iraq and Syria); it is a criminal version of the same viral phenomenon.

In the cases of ISIS and its ideological purity, evolution of culture exists in a vacuum. But that culture doesn't represent real life the way the rest of us know it: Real life still has opposing ideas and ideologies that clash. This conflict creates animosity either as the idea emerges or as the other side first sees what is brewing. If you remove the Internet from the discussion, you can draw an analogy to pre-Civil War United States: two very different ideologies living separately and distinctly with knowledge of the other but little real interaction. The primary difference is that now with every person having a voice, the sounds are louder, more immediate, and less respectful as the opposing views interact.

In a quasi-cloistered group, communication styles are evolving, language is changing, as well as ideas of what is acceptable behavior and communication style. This impact of culture is a more distilling and separating one. For example, language related to gender slowly evolved. For generations, "he" was the base pronoun used in writing; the phrase that English teachers used to describe the rule was "masculine by preference." This evolved and the use of "she" became more prevalent. With the emergence of gender issues, subcultures are pushing the introduction of new pronouns to identify people. Will the movement take hold? Only time will answer the question. Societies are living, breathing things with their own tolerances and their own resistance. They all have an immune system to protect against perceived threats—and that makes change *hard*.

There is also a profound physical change occurring in our world today. The United Nations High Commission for Refugees estimates that nearly one percent of the global population is in refugee status.[6] This is a higher percentage than it's ever been, even during World War II. This means ideas and cultural nuances from all over the world are moving to new places, and things like diet, ideology, communication styles, dress, and even tolerance are in a stew in most parts of the world. This means ideologies in the places in conflict are in a purge mode, creating a more homogenous society while at the same time diluting the homogeneity of the societies that receive the refugees. If given a choice, many of these refugees are going to the place with the best benefits and places that will allow them to create a new normal. How a society welcomes and adopts refugees will play a huge part in how this plays out. But there will be some tough dynamics when traditionally stable societies begin taking in people with different ideology and culture. Finding a way to assimilate new citizens into the "mainstream" culture will be difficult at best in our fragmented Western world, but this fragmentation is the cost of freedom of expression. If we mainstream this influx into societies and they become part of the "norm," what new things will they bring to our communication? Our style? Our body language? Societal evolution is inevitable.

Culture impacts every aspect of understanding body language. It affects how people move, even resulting in fine distinctions between many so-called universal, involuntary movements, such as raising eyebrows when you recognize another person. It also affects how you perceive the message associated with another person's body language. Your filters rooted in prejudices of different kinds and the way you project meaning took shape as a result of your culture.

Dynamics Inside a Culture

We use a simple model to depict where someone fits within a culture: the bell curve. The first thing to remember in moving a person on to the bell curve is that he may be part of many cultures or micro-cultures. Similar to members of the Ku Klux Klan, who covered their identities in white sheets, we all carry around ties to micro-cultures that are not evident when we are grouped with the mass. You will start sorting behavior as cultural, super-cultural, or sub-cultural on a model in which the "cultural" refers to the greater group you are a part of. You will routinely start placing individuals and behaviors on bell curves.

The bell curve represents a range of values. For example, ask a group of high school boys how many of them had a skinned knee at least once. Everyone will raise his hand except for the kid whose mother taped bubble wrap around his knees. Twice? Most will keep a hand up. Five times? Only a few hands will remain. The bell curve based on that information looks similar to this, and we've added the terms "sub-typical," "typical," and "super-typical" to clarify the concept.

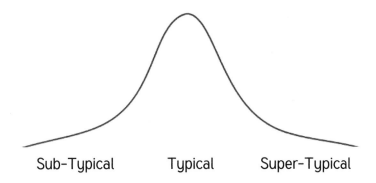

Sub-Typical   Typical   Super-Typical

In this model, anyone with a skinned knee less than twice is sub-typical; two to five times becomes the norm, and more than five times is super-typical. Is this a distorted view of the group? Sure, but it does represent one aspect of the group dynamic. It also gives us a model for further analyzing the meaning of the data and targeting something about this group to understand the group's identity. People seize on differences to create taboos and create a culture. We can overlay this into a more normal everyday situation. For example:

1. Mark Zuckerberg is super-typical in the greater understanding of American culture. A healthy 30-year-old man who lives with and is supported by his parents is sub-typical. A 45-year-old woman who works in the human resources department of a manufacturing company is typical. Are there aspects of American culture in which Mark Zuckerberg is sub-typical or labeled as a geek? Sure. This helps us to better understand why demographics and statistics can be used to make any point we want to make.

2. Within a high school group, you can easily spot the kids who are the most admired. These super-typical kids may be the athletes, cheerleaders, or student council leaders, depending on the school. Next are the masses, or the typical. In this group are the normal kids with average social skills who do not stand out among the others. Kids with poor social skills populate the last group; this may include gangly kids who are not comfortable with their quickly growing bodies. These kids are the sub-typical. The students call them names, such as "the bean" and "stick man" to remind them of this status.

In this model the super-typical have sway over the typical, who, in turn, disregard the sub-typical. They tolerate the sub-typical as part of the greater group, but given the opportunity to separate, the typical would group with the super-typical. If this is not an option, they may fragment within their own group into other micro-cultures. The typical admire and even emulate the super-typical in the hope of gaining their approval. The sub-typical hope to become typical.

In the early 1970s, a researcher from the State University of New York (SUNY) interviewed children of migrant farm workers. "What do you want to be when you grow up?" she asked. When encouraged to lift up their imaginations and hopes, most of the kids said, "Crew foreman." Very few named professions, such as a doctor or lawyer. At the time, this was an example of hoping to move to the next level up.

Today, through access to information and virtual cultural connections, fewer children of skilled labor union employees aspire to the trades. In fact, in the United States, skilled trades are desperate for new hires. It is proof of the evolution of American culture fueled by the ability to bond outside of physical constraints. It changes aspirations, but constraints on opportunities still exist. As a corollary, "virtual" doesn't equate to non-real, and cyber bullying and social pressure are no less stressful to current generations than what used to happen face-to-face. We are monkeys with machines trying to push sub-typicals or typicals down a level to make ourselves feel better.

Our primate cousins behave this way: The super-typical comprise the ruling class of chimps. The alpha-male establishes a pecking order in which he is king. All others jockey for position. The pack includes the super-typical, alpha-male and female, the masses, and the sub-typical, but the last group is barely part of the pack. Humankind repeats this model on different scales.

Do we emulate the super-typical in our subculture? Look around you at your workplace. Do you emulate the behavior of the alpha-female or male in hope of approval? Does the latest trend started by super-typical Celebrity X spark spin-offs in the population? Even if you think you are immune, would you ever comment on a fact related to a celebrity? For example, Beyoncé *almost* fell during her Super Bowl 50 half time show. Celebrity-watching has grown into a billion-dollar industry, serving the intellectual curiosity of a nation of pop culture geniuses. How typical.

By addressing this topic of culture up front, we want to arouse your awareness of how imperative it is that you ask yourself, "How important is it that I'm Japanese when trying to read that person's body language?" "How much do my Islamic beliefs affect my perception of the meaning of her gestures?" "How much does the fact that I'm a staunch Republican color my understanding of his presentation?" And as corollaries, you will ask questions such as "Am I a typical Republican?" and "Is she a typical American?"

Ape culture is simple: big alpha-male dominates; paired with alpha-female, he becomes the ruling hierarchy. Other male apes may scheme and attempt to breed part of the harem without the knowledge of the alpha-male, but alphas absolutely control social norming. At one point in our development, human culture was likely very similar to the super-typical—clearly defined.

Looking back at the Celtic kings referenced earlier in this chapter, we can see a more sophisticated model in their culture than in the ape world. The kings and their sub-chiefs were the super-typical. Going against the rules—publicized by word of mouth and personal observation—resulted in retribution. In their shaved-ape world, king and chieftains became the alpha-chimps. Consistent with their primate nature, people recognized the super-typical and began to emulate.

On the rare occasions when a "superior" member of the clan copied behavior of someone with less stature, he wanted something and determined that the copied behavior would get it for him. It could have been a style of socializing or the choice of person he took to bed.

This pattern continued to evolve throughout the ages until reaching our modern era. Looking for the super-typical, people often found them in clergy, politicians, and the wealthy; this happened for obvious reasons: The average man had no voice outside his immediate sub-group, and no means to amplify his voice. In fact, he didn't even know the words to amplify, which is why the literate clergy represented a ruling class of its own. The wealthy achieved that status through connections, and belonged to an established structure with implied power.

As media has proliferated and communication has become ubiquitous, these relationships have taken a dramatic turn. Let's briefly explore American culture as a way of understanding how cultures evolve, which will prepare you to make the intimate link between the resultant culture and body language.

Even within a culture generally described as "American," there are divisions you need to consider, to ask yourself how typical, super-typical, or sub-typical you are within those. In the United States, for example, a big part of our culture is a sense of entitlement. From its inception, the American culture espoused a belief that all men are created equal. Although often not as valid in practice as in theory, it was an American ideal. At that time, few people had the means or savvy to use media in presenting such ideas across the colonies. Enough of them held a belief that the fledgling country needed to allow common people an opportunity to succeed, so the message hit the streets.

With its independence, the United States established a unique culture that consisted of disparate groups, each of which assimilated in its own way. We have often referred to this as the melting pot. The melting-pot concept implies that, slowly as they cook in the fires of a national heat, the characteristics of "typical" change based on the percentage of the population each group represents. Each person entering the country assimilates to his or her new home and decides exactly how to fit in.

Southern planters and Northern industrialists, each with their own distinct ideas about what it meant to be American, were the super-typical. These ideas were shared by enough of the respective population to lose more than 600,000 American lives during the war. The war was called "The Civil War by Northerners" and "The War Between the States" by Southerners. Do we believe that the super-typical merely ordered these people to fight? No more than we believe the average Southerners lived similarly to Scarlett O'Hara, the fictional heroine of *Gone with the Wind*. These people had come to identify with very different pictures of what it meant to be American, and The Civil War was the occasion to reconcile those two pictures. This is hard-fought social norming.

As a result of this conflict, the emancipated slave emerged as a new class of American citizen. Particularly in areas where they had been slaves, these people of color were treated as the sub-typical. The Americans who had gone to war and lost that war would vilify them and, in some cases, even deny them rights. Think of the chimp model again: A super-typical alpha who is dropped to typical status will become more than disdainful of the sub-typical. This would prove to be one of the most complex assimilations in American history.

Here is what's going on behind the curtain: As a result of a melting-pot culture, some sub-groups lay outside cultural norms. These people should enjoy the rights of the greater culture, but don't. The nature of humans is to deny those who are not the typical or super-typical as much as possible. The sub-typical receive different treatment from the typical or super-typical.

The super-typical people of the day, principally politicians and activists, tried to correct these wrongs through writings and speeches. Which do you think carried the most power, even in an age before mass-media: the typical or super-typical? Imagine the presence of a 6-foot, 5-inch Abraham Lincoln delivering the Gettysburg Address. By visual contact and word-of-mouth, Lincoln rose to the throne of alpha-chimp.

After this, American culture expanded steadily to include large groups of Mexican immigrants, Pacific Islanders, Inuit, and many others. Assimilation can be painful, especially for those assimilating. Each new group brought new flavors to the melting pot. Meanwhile, the belief that all men are created equal was tested.

The Great Depression hit America at the time of a fledgling technology: radio. A new kind of American politician evolved: the media-savvy politician. Now, not only the verbal, but also the vocal portion of a president's speech could be experienced first-hand.

This time of "doing without" for Americans offered fertile ground for President Franklin Delano Roosevelt when he came up with the New Deal and, through radio, spoke to average Americans in their own homes about entitlement. Could anyone become more super-typical than a president with a plan for *you* in your own living room? Without an image of FDR in the wheelchair, Americans heard only his message. Still, photos provided the only source of body language to most people. He was the alpha in living rooms across the nation telling Americans how much they deserved—just for living. A new sense of entitlement flourished as the new media broadcasting it became ubiquitous.

After Roosevelt held an omnipresent power with his voice, John F. Kennedy held it with his face. He personally, but also through the legacy of his presidency, engendered a lively sense of entitlement. Is there any doubt as to why Americans were inconsolable when they watched their quintessential alpha die at the hands of some nondescript upstart one fall afternoon? This nation with the perception of super power had its most alpha male destroyed by a sub-typical hiding in a storage room. Such ignominy was inconceivable. It is likely the reason why JFK's death still fuels the greatest conspiracy theories in the United States today.

Returning to the historical context, people who endured sustained denial of the basic rights of the typical, as well as their supporters, got angry. The United States began to develop a conscience and a culture that recognized this. Enter media powered by new technologies. They offered the super-typical an opportunity to redress in ways FDR's generation could not imagine.

African-Americans, members of the sub-typical, had little access. But there were super-typical, African-Americans as well, who had both drive and access, and a conscience to stand with them. Their efforts launched the Civil Rights movement, and the course was set to create a culture that tolerated differences in the framework of equal rights under the law.

And then came an ideological hijacking. More media translated into more media access by more people. Americans could become super-typical simply by being on camera or in print. It is impossible to sustain an identity based on standing in front of the camera when the camera makes every part of a person's life a subject for coverage. Even if he could maintain this status, it is much more desirable to become super-typical in a subculture of the sub-typical.

These new super-typical citizens understood that they needed causes to maintain their identity. A common way to forge it was by spotlighting areas in which their sub-typical neighbors struggled, by raising the flag of entitlement as it pertained to food, healthcare, or education, for example. Others who became super-typical because of their talent (including a "talent" such as inherited wealth), were seduced by their own image. But unlike Narcissus admiring his own reflection in the pool, much of the population joined them in the love fest. Who could blame these celebrities for developing a sense of superiority in multiple aspects of life? Through precedent, people gave them the right to display that superiority by advising the ordinary people in matters of lifestyle, domestic politics, and even international relations. They, too, saw the need to adopt causes to maintain their identity.

This situation, in which celebrities with a range of mental abilities and wisdom make pronouncements on social change, results in three outcomes:

1. **It helps a culture of victims to take shape.** Playboy model, comedian, and actress Jenny McCarthy and her diatribe against the

vaccination schedule for children are a prime example. With no scientific basis for her campaign against certain childhood vaccinations—in fact, what she says is nonsense that splatters on the window of science—she asserts that there is a link between autism and vaccinations. This has engendered a culture of victims linked to her assertion that anyone with an autistic child who received routine immunization should ask whether or not vaccines caused the autism. She calls on parents of autistic children to blame something external rather than their own genes as the cause of their child's developmental problems. She has become super-typical as a person in a small group who desperately seeks answers. Whether the answers are real or not isn't important; she simply needs to be the voice and ask questions.

2. **It raises the celebrity status of those super-typical people who have exhibited righteous indignation over the treatment of the sub-typical.** Bob Geldof was the lead singer of a quasi-popular Irish band called The Boomtown Rats when he put together the largest simulcast live event in TV history. His Live Aid concert on July 13, 1985, showed hours of stars performing to raise money to feed all those starving kids in Ethiopia—the ones who would survive and thrive if only they had some cash. Geldof skyrocketed to global fame overnight, despite the fact that Live Aid's £150 million in revenues had nowhere to go because of the political and military situation in Ethiopia. Ultimately, it was distributed between non-governmental organizations (NGOs) and the corrupt government. It's probably the most misguided humanitarian effort in history, but at least for a while the world knew who Bob Geldof was. Did he have good intentions? Not important; the outcome would be the same.

3. **The concept of tolerance assumes a distorted meaning: "whatever." As in, "do whatever you want," and "be whatever you want."** After leaving his television show *Two and a Half Men*, actor Charlie Sheen launched a multi-city tour called "My Violent Torpedo of Truth: Defeat is Not an Option." A haphazard solo act with cameo appearances by his two blonde "goddesses," Sheen strutted and ranted, inviting not only tolerance, but also support from his fans for his right to do "whatever" *and* keep his children. The month following his tour, he got an HIV-positive diagnosis. Whatever.

When something like this happens, no one aspires to become the typical. Remember the bell curve? People in a culture with these pressures now aspire to the super-typical *only*—they want to be super-typical in their *own* micro-culture, whatever that is—and they contort their behavior to get there. They hang on to anything that makes them special, that distinguishes them as unique.

Alternately, with zero understanding of the other culture, people see something sexy and opt to self-appoint as members of that culture. This is a shortcut to becoming super-typical in a less-cool group. This has always played out with the average high school kid who learned about some new exotic music or career field no one ever heard of and suddenly becoming a huge fan or wanting to become an "X" (tattoo artist, data architect, and so on). Today, the difference is that people are doing some of it well into adulthood by becoming the local guy who is going to be the next Kanye West, even if he is 29 and working at the Pizza Hut with no chance of meeting Kim Kardashian.

Voilá: The result is America as a jellybean jar rather than a melting pot. Create more celebrity by being different, and in the process sacrifice "American culture" by glorifying uniqueness. The paradox that also affects thinking and behavior, of course, is that "American culture" affords rights and privileges based on the ideology that we are all created equal.

We keep circling back to the discussion of entitlement. Most of us feel we have a right to the basics, not only of survival, but a quality of life. We have a right to personal mobility and choices at the grocery store. We have the right of appeal if a court case doesn't go our way. And in many peoples' minds, we have the right to yell profanities at a politician, preacher, or police officer we hate. Depending on who we are, that sense of entitlement can have vastly different implications, and others in the world might view some of them as bizarre, even though Americans are not alone in feeling this is a right. Watch Greece unravel on television as average Greeks take to the street in sometimes violent protest that their entitlements have been cut in austerity programs, even though very few of them pay the taxes they owe to fund those entitlements. Combine the concepts of "subjugated" and "born with a spectrum of rights" and the result is a super-entitled victim.

When we go overseas, we are often lumped together as "the ugly American," because people abroad recognize our sense of entitlement and may make a sweeping assumption about how it affects our gestures and language. They don't necessarily take into consideration that, depending on how strong the sense of entitlement is, an American's reaction to a violation can range from the obvious to the subtle, from purposeful affectations to movements emanating from the subconscious.

Probably more than any other cultural group, Americans suffer from culture shock when traveling abroad because of perceived homogeneity of the entire North American continent. Most Americans from Monterey to Manhattan share at least a common language and jargon for finding what they need. When this does not work, there is a huge displacement of expectations.

Most Americans expect to walk into a government office in the United States and get an answer in English. Is this a reasonable expectation? Today, yes. In times to come, when the majority of the jellybeans do not speak English as a first language, maybe not.

A hard-won homogeneity of culture in the United States will disappear as the predominately Germanic culture dies off. Speculate about a time when Americans are primarily Hispanic and the typical citizen becomes a Spanish speaker. Residents of California and New Mexico don't have to speculate. The U.S. Census Bureau and Pew Research Center concur that the Hispanic/Latino population of both states has surpassed non-Hispanic whites. Pew also projects that Texas is next in the near future.[7] As the process of racial and ethnic shifting continues to evolve, what happens to new immigrants from other regions of the world? The jellybean jar changes labels to the Spanish equivalent and the new ethnic group feels victimized until either every sign in every building is in their language, too, or the new Hispanic typical says, "Learn the language of the land." This sense of entitlement is not free. Who pays for the interpreters?

The days have passed when Americans identified with singular role models, such as John Wayne. Modern heroes tend to be big names in their microcultures—skateboarder, rock star, tattoo artist—and we look to media and advertising that feature them for our cultural norming. With the proliferation of media, every micro-culture can have its own spokesman (super-typical) on the air. Becoming similar to those people validates our attempts to be unique; we no longer look at them as outcasts. Because the super-typical "must" be right, their image is the image of what it means to be American, not only to us but also to the rest of the world as well. Arabs in Iraq watch *The Brady Bunch*; Greg learned this from first-hand experience and also heard it from Army buddies who served there in the most recent war. Imagine how repeated exposure to the Brady kids' sibling rivalry and family vacations in Hawaii affects how Iraqis view Americans. No wonder they would be a little surprised when someone who looks similar Peter Brady walks down the street with an M16 strapped to him.

Now, let's move to the influence of super-typical on the typical, but on a smaller scale.

One factor that contributes to the different forms of response is the influences of subgroups within a culture. Why are Texans seen as brash by other fellow Americans even though we're all part of the "same culture"? Their heritage and accomplishments shaped behavior patterns. Texans carved an environment in the wilderness from nothing, rounding up their cattle and introducing organization where there was none. They claim the distinction of being the only American state to ever be an independent nation. The super-typicals of Texas, such as Stephen Austin, Sam Houston, Davy Crockett, and Jim Bowie earned larger-than-life status. So Texans have an ingrained pride about being tough; they are a force to be reckoned with and traditionally have a fierce sense of entitlement. Add to that the fact that many of the original immigrants were Germans, who have a guttural language that people from Latin-language areas hear as harsh. So, how did people with a contrasting background, say, East Coast English, tend to describe Texans? They strutted. They were loud. Their gestures were too big. This became the heritage of the modern Texan. Just like the mentality of the Old South impacts the psyche of the modern Southern child, or like the magnitude of the 9/11 attacks on the World Trade Center will affect generations of New Yorkers, so too does the larger-than-life Texan impact a child of The Lone Star State. Though much of the old culture is gone, it is still echoed in the behavior of people who call themselves Texans. If you think it is dead, think again. Greg recently attended the grand opening of a company's manufacturing facility in Texas. Among the guests were the assistant to the U.S. Senator from Texas who presented a U.S. flag to the facility. The State Representative also presented a state flag, along with the commentary, "This is like the U.S. flag. It has stars, but bigger, bolder, and more significant." That was a clear reference to the feeling of Texans of their place in the union.

Almost invariably, you will observe distinctive body language associated with a group, as large as Texas or as small as a high-school cheerleading squad. Even temporary groups, such as a fraternity pledge class, a clique of pot-smoking kids at school, a street gang, or a team of gung-ho salesmen, will create unique "tribal customs." In contrast, a lot of gestures common within foreign cultures may go unnoticed by us or may arouse an inappropriate reaction because we have no idea what they really mean. These cultural norms are direct responses to social pressure, both positive and negative. Although the super-typical may get away with introducing something new, an average Joe will be chastised for the attempt. Similar to the alpha-chimp, human societies have a way of forcing compliance.

Rites of Passage and Social Norming

Although associated with particular cultures, people in the culture may or may not even acknowledge that certain common practices fall into the "rites of passage category." Rites of passage are connected with body language because they affect how a culture evolves.

Passing a driver's test is a rite of passage in the United States. Soon after that, the urge to walk simply to get someplace often subsides. It is rare for Americans to walk on a regular basis unless they're city dwellers. Does this show in our body language? Absolutely.

Consider how the following extreme examples affect the body language, temporarily or even permanently, of the people who have experienced them.

- **Scarification:** Whether it's done by cutting or burning, this is a ceremonial injuring of a person in such a way that the scar tissue forms a particular design. Depending on the culture, it could mark the person as an adult male, a female who's ready and willing to bear children, a criminal, a part of a tribe, and so on.

- **Starting to wear make-up and nail polish (without mom's help):** American girls definitely use this as a sign of being grown up. Using nail polish and make-up of their own choosing means that these girls think they're ready to make a few other decisions without their mother's help—and the body language shows it.

Everywhere around you, rites of passage occur daily and give rise to social norming. The effect of social norming is: Every time you repeat a ritual with a group, you become more cohesive with the group. These rites of passage traditionally occur at certain times in a person's assimilation with the group and can be formal or informal. If rites of passage are rushed, delayed, or foregone, the consequences can range from insignificant to dire. A son who lives with his parents until 25 and suddenly becomes famous may have minor repercussions as an adult, while the child whose sexual maturity is rushed because she's competing in beauty pageants at 5 years old may have a difficult adult life. Expectations—emotions that feed entitlements—will affect behavior.

In considering rites of passage, don't overlook any human interaction. Rites of passage are created to separate you from one group and bond you to another forever, changing the way you think. They may be elaborate and codified or spur of the moment. From circumcision to baptism to your first pair of bifocals, each has an effect forever on the way you perceive yourself. They summon the sub-typical chimp to emulate the alpha.

At an early age, American boys learn restroom etiquette as they observe dad, big brother, or uncle behaving "like a man" in the restroom. (For many young boys, the rite of passage underlying this is that they finally get to use the restroom with Dad instead of Mom.) This behavior relates closely to rituals similar to the secret handshake of the Freemasons: Every time a person participates in some activity, it leaves residual memory. In some cases, it even becomes muscle memory, because when it is done enough times, the action becomes involuntary.

Exercise

Make a short list of formal cultural norming practices in place around you that affect how you behave. A couple examples are:

- If you attend a church with services dominated by ritual (the Catholic Mass, for instance), what behaviors are required of you? Do any of those behaviors surface when you're around the same people, even in a setting outside of church?
- The medieval recreations require strict adherence to certain courtly behaviors based on Victorian ideals and battlefield practices. A deviation from that will likely get you booted out of the group, or publicly chastised.

Here's another thought to get you started: Maryann used to work for a 30-person company that adopted a no-smoking policy in the workplace in the early 1990s, before it was a common practice. All six smokers who worked there eventually found themselves taking breaks about the same time and hanging out at the same spot outside the building. They grew into their own sub-culture within the organization and established social norming practices, such as when and where to take breaks, body language to signal "it's time to take a break," or "I wish it were time to take a break."

If you're part of five groups, you'll have social mimicry in all five of them, even ones as informal as the smokers' group. By the way, can you imagine the additional social pressure each one had to remain a smoker after years, or even a few months, of repeating this pattern Monday through Friday? As this shows, then, you can have very narrow social norms, as well as very broad ones, such as those associated with your service in the military or your national heritage. For example, people in the United States put their hands over their hearts when they pledge allegiance to the flag. Here is another type of example: Finnish people are known for staying within the law even when it comes to small transgressions like jaywalking and slightly exceeding the speed limit. At first glance, you might think this cultural body language is a reflection of voluntary social norming, but it isn't. Finland has income-based penalties for violations of laws; that is, your fine for speeding is a percentage of your salary.

These types of social norms and cultural rituals are an overlay for everyone who is alive. In reading body language, therefore, you absolutely have to consider them. Think in terms of what distinctive traits or marks you can identify based on how they identify each other.

In practicing your identification skills, pay attention to what people do at all kinds of events associated with a culture. Whether they are rites of passage, such as a wedding or funeral, or entertainment, they showcase ritual behavior of that culture. Weddings and funerals provide formal examples of how people in that group display love and grief as an overlay to the involuntary ways that all human beings express love and grief. Sporting events exhibit how people in a culture demonstrate support. Do they cheer and applaud their own team more than they boo and throw beer cans at the opponent? The differences are the basis for sub-cultural stereotypes, such as Philadelphia Phillies fans, who seem to boo with their whole bodies. As for Hollywood culture, the Academy Awards are a good occasion to see how ritual is not always synchronous with an actor's real emotions. Most of the people on the red carpet try hard to behave in a stately manner and to accept their awards with dignity. You can see a lot of glitchy behavior in this crowd because they try to use rituals of the event to disguise their true feelings.

This norming criterion is also a good way to determine who is not part of a tribe. The guest at a funeral who is bored, and shows it, probably isn't a close member of the grieving family. The Phillies fan who applauds when Yoenis Céspedes hits a home run for the Mets needs to leave town before he's run out of it. When you practice this evaluation, are you profiling?

Now that we've gone down that controversial path, we will tell you that you will think differently about other people if you absorb the lessons in this book and practice R.E.A.D. Depending on your level of adoption of these techniques, the information in this book will change your social norms.

Exercise

Tell people you are reading a book on body language. See what they do. When they respond with some combination of curiosity and concern—and you read it—say, "They said you would do that." Keep watching, because the next response will be predictable too! As you do this, your own social norms are changing a little bit at a time.

The Shock of a New Culture

Culture is a way of connecting with our fellow chimps, and identifying the differences between us and them, when we run into a new breed of chimp. We have been conditioned from birth to behave in certain ways in response to stimulus, and our micro-cultures regulate that response, even from infancy. An alpha, parent or other, dominates that micro-culture.

Every time we react to stimulus and adopt new behaviors presented by a parent we are adopting the culture of our family. This goes on with limited incursions from other bands of chimps. Then, one day, the inevitable happens. We come face-to-face with new chimps—similar to a baby sitter—and new cultural norms. In the case of a sitter, the new alpha is akin to a captor: Things will return to normal when she leaves. We learn this quickly.

The most profound culture shock in a child's life is more likely daycare or the first day of school. Now this child must deal with a new person who is solidly alpha. He must adopt the ways of this alpha while in her presence. The food, the lighting, the blankets—suddenly the child's perception of his place in the hierarchy goes into a blender. To make it equally difficult, the child must retain an understanding of what the alpha in the nest wants. This is profound culture shock. Most people cannot remember it, but they certainly recognize it in their own children.

This same thing takes affect when you walk into a new office, new school, or new relationship. The difference, in most cases, is that you speak the same language, eat the same food, and have at least some gesturing and acceptable behaviors in common. You see and identify or become the new alpha, and the culture adapts.

Sometimes you get caught between cultures until you're really sure what all the "rules" of the new culture are. A great place to watch this cultural evolution is school, whether it's first grade or college. You utter sounds, wear clothes, add body adornments, and make gestures that attract those we want to attract. Some of the efforts are very much on the conscious level and some of them are not. Often, until you're sure who it is you want to attract—and this applies to people in whom you're interested in sexually as well as people you want as non-sexual companions—you might send mixed messages. You wear the clothes of the type of people you aim to spend time with, but may not have captured their vocabulary or cadence of speech, for example.

Through this adaptation we all learn to be successful organisms within a culture, whether a micro-culture or super-culture. Exposure is the key. We adapt skills that work, and we orchestrate their use with other skills that we learn as we go. When we move to a new place and the skills no longer produce the desired result, we have no concept or location to store that information. We start to grasp for something that will work. The chimp in us wins. We instinctively know that emulating the alpha's behavior is better than not.

In *Rangers Lead the Way*, former U.S. Army Ranger Dean Hohl talks about the cultural differences among the newbies he entered training with, and how and why the Ranger culture submerged when they were on duty.

The first day I got to my Ranger unit, I was with a group of people who were "home." Up until that point, I was in training, so I was always carrying my bags with me. I didn't have much in the way of personal clothing—maybe one pair of jeans and a T-shirt. But these guys who had been in the Ranger unit for so long had settled in and made a home, with clothing and other personal items. I looked around and there was a guy in a cowboy hat, another one in biker leathers, one guy looked like a preppie from back East, another had on a T-shirt picturing a heavy metal band, another guy came across as a hillbilly. They spent their off hours doing wildly different things. Socially, they didn't pretend to have anything in common. I was dumbfounded by the differences between them. Though these differences were sharp, they became irrelevant when we were on a mission. When we put on our Ranger uniform and heard Captain Thomas say, "This is your objective," we were a team.

...Ranger training and culture...translate into patterns that are more focused on practical, measurable outcomes.[8]

Because culture involves choice, a person can suddenly change his body language in response to culture shock. Part of the change may be mimicking what appear to be accepted gestures, and part of it may be subduing what comes naturally because it seems out of place. Take, for instance, the habit of crossing the legs to make yourself comfortable. Many American men cross legs in the figure-4 style, that is, one leg crossing the other with the ankle or calf resting on the knee. Men from the Middle East would not assume this posture for two reasons: one is seating styles, and the other is that showing the soles of the feet is insulting. The pressure on an American man negotiating with Middle Eastern people would be to avoid that body posture and adopt something more appropriate for the context.

Culture shock results after moving from one culture to another. It commonly involves four stages.

1. Euphoria over being in a new environment.
2. Irritation that things are different.
3. Adaptation to the new culture, which is typically a process rather a quick transformation.
4. Full recovery/full adaptation.

Some of the adjustments that a culture-shocked traveler might make are the proximity at which you stand to someone, the amount of time you look into a stranger's eyes, and whether or not you sit with your legs crossed. For example, after haggling with a vendor at a Mexican market, Maryann suddenly got a big hug from the woman who had just sold her a necklace. That kind of close contact, even with strangers, is common in Latin American cultures. If that had happened in Philadelphia, it would have been weird.

Because culture impacts every part of our being, from cadence to how close we stand to people, and the broader our understanding of other cultures, the less likely we are to suffer culture shock. The more exposed we are to new things, the fuller our repertoire of what is acceptable, or even normal. And as we age, we all compartmentalize and create specific strategies for adaptation.

This big influencer of culture will affect every action a person is capable of doing. Think about your young self first learning to wave at someone with your middle finger. How long did that last before your Micro-culture Alpha (aka your mother or father) put a stop to it? Culture cannot add to the things you are capable of, but rather add meaning to what you can do, in turn allowing you to communicate with another person or group more effectively. The problem is that the signals need to be understood. Think about every element of culture and its impact as you start on your journey of cataloging what you see.

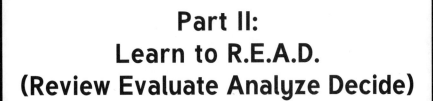

Part II:
Learn to R.E.A.D.
(Review Evaluate Analyze Decide)

3

Review From Scalp to Soles

All of us are born with roughly the same abilities to use our bodies to communicate, and yet those abilities result in some remarkable differences in the way we express ourselves. You know a lot about your culture and sub-cultures, and something about other cultures to which you've been exposed. You will need to apply that knowledge when you start to read body language. For example, you can't simply assume that because you were born with hands, arms, legs, and feet that you have the ability to communicate in Plains Indian Sign Language. The Native American hand talker communicated in a context where others understood him. Setting matters; that's why we begin with a look at the context in which communication is occurring in order to read and understand body language.

The "review" part of R.E.A.D. is all about intake and there are two ways to do it: macro and micro. When you take a macro view of body language, you go for the big picture—context and elements that compose it—whereas a micro view is a focus on details. You need both in order to grasp and use the R.E.A.D. system.

By "intake" we mean try not to judge or overlay; just open your eyes, look, listen, smell. This is about taking in as much data as possible. No shortcuts allowed. Don't worry; we will ask you to use your very specific knowledge to fill in gaps in the Decide section.

A discussion about how to develop a macro perspective precedes the scalp-to-soles look at individual movements: It alerts you to the fact that you can only be good at reading and using body language if you see individual movements within a given environment. There are multiple values to this. One is differentiating between an ordinary setting and an iconic one. Another is that you are tuned in to the relative importance of a person of having control over environment *versus* responding to it. A third is that you grasp how easy it can be to use location to manipulate someone else's body language.

All the World's a Stage

William Shakespeare could have been writing part of a body language book when he penned the opening of a famous monologue from *As You Like It*:

All the world's a stage,
And all the men and women merely players;
They have their exits and their entrances,
And one man in his time plays many parts.

Consider this: Every time you enter a room, exit a building onto a city street, or get into a car on a roller coaster, you are on stage. Did you plan your move, or was this something you didn't mean to do, or you did it before you were ready? Did you intend to go to that particular room or street or roller coaster car, or do you feel surprised by fact that you're there?

In theater, there are (theoretically, anyway) no surprises to the actors on stage. Everyone knows where everything is and when changes will occur. They are in an established four-dimensional grid, meaning length, width, depth, and time. This creates a condition wherein actors can conduct intentional emotional signaling to convey a message. Interrogators do the same thing: They coordinate elements of their environment so that everything, down to a breath, sends an intended message. In the theater, when some set piece is out of place, missing, or damaged, it potentially disrupts the timing of line delivery and interaction. All of a sudden, the world of "no surprises" offers a surprise. The same is true for humans in everyday life.

Author and organizational consultant Jim McCormick (*The First Time Manager*) is a friend of ours who has made more than 4,500 skydives and holds 10 world records in skydiving. The act of jumping out of a perfectly good airplane is about as routine for him as it can get for anyone. And yet, when he realized on jump number 4,270 that the parachute rigger had installed his new canopy backward (when it opened, he was moving 30 miles per hour in the wrong direction) a relatively routine experience was suddenly full of surprises. Like an actor in a dialogue with someone who introduced lines from another play, he was faced with the need to "re-normalize" his situation. And like a well-trained actor, he did. If this happened on the fifth jump of his life, the body language would likely have been very different. Simply watching Jim in the air moving 30 miles per hour backward and seeming relatively calm would send a message not planned by Jim at that moment, but certainly it would project a great deal about his state of mind.

Where something occurs is important, not only because it can indicate why the other person's body language is occurring, but also because it can impact and alter your review of that body language. Our minds are complex, filled with active sub-routines that project and fill in blanks based on past experience and fear of the unknown.

Depending on whether a location—the "set" in theater and film—is ordinary or iconic, perception of another person's body language and intentions will be affected. The following story is an example of how this can play out. Hanns Scharff was the German Luftwaffe interrogator whose techniques of connecting positively with prisoners have shaped Western nonphysical interrogation practices in modern times. Prisoners brought to Scharff at Dulag Luft POW Camp expected harsh, Gestapo-style treatment. Instead, they met a man who spoke English fluently and was skilled at using psychological levers to draw out of them far more than name, rank, and serial number. Sharff's method relied both on an ordinary, rather than iconic, location and a casual communication style that would not have worked well in the context of a typical Nazi interrogation.

When prisoners arrived at the camp, they were held in solitary confinement. When they were brought to Scharff, he took them outside for walks in the woods and talked with them about their home town, family, and so on. By taking that approach, he relieved their sense of isolation and at the same time he avoided exposing them to the iconic setting of an interrogation room. The prisoners didn't have the symbolic picture in their head of the small table, two chairs, bright light, and bare walls. They didn't feel as though they were being interrogated, and the result was that Scharff psychologically disarmed them.

Knowing how to use an iconic setting can also bring results, of course. Someone working in a funeral home knows that she has opportunities to take advantage of the iconic surroundings to up-sell. Better casket! More flowers! A guest book with the deceased's name embossed in gold!

Whether the location for your interaction is ordinary or iconic, certain expectations come with each. So in the case of Hanns Scharff, prisoners lost their perception of threat so they behaved differently from their behavior in an iconic interrogation environment. And in the case of the funeral home, grieving people faced with the immediate need to make funeral arrangements often respond with open wallets to the "helpful" sales pitches of funeral home staff.

Your job as you become skilled in the R.E.A.D. system is to begin processing the elements of location like a child: Be curious about everything. Question everything.

This can be especially tough to do when faced with an ordinary location as opposed to an iconic one. We get so accustomed to certain environments that we tune out everything we see; it's how we overlook things. People are often bitten by rattlesnakes because they step on them without having seen them. Not wanting a confrontation, the snake doesn't rattle because it prefers to rely on its camouflage to keep from being noticed; the rattle would give away its position. The Loachapoka, Alabama, resident going for a walk near his house is used to his surroundings; he isn't on alert so he doesn't notice the snake—until the snake bites him.

As a final note to this location discussion, let's return to the notion of expected, or intended, events that occur in a location *versus* surprising, or unintended, events. If you intend to be in a particular location at a particular time and moving in a particular way, you are exactly like the actor or dancer on a stage. Your precise movements even have a special name ("blocking"), which reflects the director's vision for the production. Your responses are essentially programmed.

However, if you don't intend to be a particular location at a particular time, your presence in that environment at that moment creates a different kind of stimulus-response interaction. Where am I? Who are these people? What are they doing? What are these objects? Your brain is very busy trying to ascertain relationships, expectations, options, and the next steps.

Greg saw a man who appeared to be homeless sitting outside a grocery store parking lot in an area where houses sat on anywhere from one to 15 acres. The bedraggled man held a sign that said "Hungry." People had to drive past him to buy food, so he probably engendered a lot of guilt in some of the grocery store customers. He chose his stage carefully and probably came a long way to get there since homeless people don't usually hang out in that area.

There is a big difference between the homeless man's level of intent in being in that location and a poor man having his car break down there. If the unkempt man were standing next to an old clunker with the hood up at that same parking lot, he might still encounter relatively well-off people with compassion, but triggering that compassion was an accident. The homeless man with the intent to be near the grocery store should have fewer surprises than the man who was stranded there.

Greg used a combination of these location-related elements—ordinary *versus* iconic, expected *versus* surprising—in coaching personnel at Trane, an Ingersoll Rand company. He was training them in negotiation and playing the role of a particularly difficult contact. The participants were sent to meet with him one by one. He ensured the location was uncomfortable, such as under the stairs near a boiler room, and added the challenge of having to trek to get to the location. He also created stimulus along the way, such as blocking off a corridor that would provide direct access or locking a door. Participants remembered their session as particularly rough and full of harsh language—none of which was true! Greg made sure the conversation was polite, even though it was also direct, as is his style. In the trek to the meeting the blank spaces in the narrative to come were filled with the participants' own dark thoughts about what was ahead. The result was a distortion of facts and what happened.

This kind of manipulation related to location happens all the time. At this phase of learning the R.E.A.D. system, it's important to be aware of it. Later on, it will be important for you to be able to use it.

The final piece of the discussion on the world as a stage involves things we add to the set and the players: properties (*aka* props) and costumes. The same issue of intended versus unintended is in play. The following story is a simple example: Maryann once had the role of Eliza Doolittle in a production of *Pygmalion*, the comedy behind the famous musical *My Fair Lady*. At every rehearsal, the props people had placed a box of chocolates on the set, so that at the right moment, Eliza's mentor Henry Higgins could pop a chocolate into her mouth to shut her up. On one of the performance evenings, someone forgot to place the chocolates. The actor playing Higgins appeared to pick up something from a table and cup his hand over Maryann's face. She recognized this immediately as air, not chocolate, but his movement—with the same timing as if he'd had a chocolate in his hand—immediately turned an unintended event into an intended event.

A speaker whose laser pointer dies during a very technical presentation or a football player who can't find his lucky bicep band are both facing the same kind of prop sabotage that could derail their performance. Their body language might leak stress instead of confidence and suddenly, their hours of diligent practice seem to be worthless. In each case, the items were chosen because they helped the "actors" do their job for an audience. Without them, the "actor" felt crippled in his communication. The prop may be intended for actual use to support the actor's message (the laser pointer) or to satisfy the actor's personal needs (the bicep band). Regardless, the unintended absence of it becomes a stimulus and creates reactionary body language in the actor.

Costuming can be even more complex: It projects what's on the inside of the person as well as reinforces the external expression of a message. Costuming tells the audience, which could be an auditorium full of technology geeks, "I am worth listening to because..." Steve Jobs in a simple black shirt and pants broadcast the message to Apple aficionados: "This is about the technology in my hand; it's not about a $7,000 Brioni suit." The costuming also reflected the thoughts and emotion inside him; they shaped his passion to create and share life-changing technology.

A costume designer dressing an actor playing a homeless person might omit or overdo an element that would make it completely realistic, because the point of the costume is to send a message, not necessarily replicate what is on the street. The costumer relies on iconic images to communicate ideas. The real homeless person's costume is created by nature and not a professional designer. The details are never wrong, unlike a costume, which might be off the mark if the costumer chooses inappropriate icons.

Costuming has a vital role in conveying messages and, again, when we get to the discussion of how to use all of the elements of expression to control conversation, affect the perception others have of you, and exert influence, we will delve into this a bit more.

Individual Movements

Many pieces of body language are an amalgamation of small signs and movements, both voluntary and involuntary. Jointly and separately, eyebrows, eyes, mouth, skin tone, limbs, fingers, and toes can convey emotions. Think of these bits of body language as the words in a sentence: It makes a lot of sense if you know all the words, but you're only guessing if you have every other word.

To get good at reading body language, go out and do the "R" over and over. Open your eyes and ears. Turn off your biased, over-analytical brain and observe the way a child observes. A toddler sees objects and actions in a more standalone way than adults, who go to extraordinary means to make connections. He has no preexisting framework to overlay his observations on to, so he's a much better collector of pure body language than older, well-socialized people. If you place a wrapped box on the table in front of a young child capable of speech, the questions are endless. As you get older, you answer the questions for yourself, assuming you know what everything means.

So as you dive into the following lists, suspend your adult brain, just as we asked you to do with an evaluation of location. When it comes to movement, it will help if you twist your face into the positions we describe; watch your arms and legs in the mirror as you mimic postures. Watch other people assume these shapes with their face and body—but just to collect information. No judgment is allowed at this stage. Look for similarities, look for differences, and that's it.

It will be easier for you to remove your filters—your blinders—from the "E," "A," and "D" parts of the process after you get good at "R." In a way, this is similar to practicing the fundamental moves of a sport before going out to play a game because you want to develop a muscle memory that supports consistent performance. This top-to-bottom look at body language has two parts:

1. A look at the isolated movements and responses of body.
2. A discussion of how clothes, accessories, body art, and gadgets play a role in your review process. The review is a scan that gives you the puzzle pieces that will come together in a future picture.

This is nothing more than a laundry list to make you aware and open your eyes to some basic concepts. You will never look at yourself or anyone else the same way. We will later address the holistic view, and give you ways to tie it all together so you can read body language.

Super-Physical Communication

All humans share some communication traits, regardless of culture, gender, or language. We explore these in depth later, but for now, focus on essential concepts so the detailed list of body movements in this chapter gets you thinking about how individual gestures might fit into a meaningful, complete picture.

- **Illustrators:** Signals used to punctuate a statement. Examples are finger pointing; head bobbing; batoning with the hand, arm, or head; and arm outstretched with the palm up, as if to suggest you are giving something. This is the mind punctuating its thoughts.
- **Regulators:** Signals used to control another person's speech, movement, or other communication. Examples are putting a hand up similar to a stop sign; putting a finger to the lips to ask for silence; and moving the hand quickly in a circle as a way of saying, "Speed it up."
- **Adaptors:** Signals used to release stress, to adjust the body as a way to increase the comfort level. Examples are hand-wringing,

neck rubbing, and curling the toes. People often develop idiosyncratic adaptors; they can also look very different depending on whether a man or a woman is doing them. (We'll explore these elements later.) Adaptors are the way we humans make the unfamiliar familiar.

- **Barriers:** Postures and movements we use to create space. Examples include standing behind a table, turning sideways, and sometimes crossing arms while in conversation. Everyone has seen someone sitting smugly behind a desk appearing confident and secure. Our primitive ancestors knew the value of such "barriering" long before we had desks, and they left us a legacy of natural techniques using only the body. Whether designed consciously or simply ritualistically, they provide individual space.

These concepts will help us speak a common language as we spotlight body movements and reactions from scalp to sole.

Forehead

We use our faces, 'the organ of expression" in Desmond Morris' terms, in ways that we rarely realize. Despite the variations, there are some standard expressions associated with the face; by no means are the ones that follow a comprehensive list. However, it does capture fundamental pieces of facial body language.

The billboard you call your forehead allows you to demonstrate the very inner workings of your mind. As a result, the forehead gives residuals, that is, it shows what you have been showing. "At 50, everyone has the face he deserves," wrote novelist George Orwell in 1949. Based on body language observation, Orwell was right. He is referring to the contours around the mouth and eyes, particularly the ones that indicate how much your face has expressed sadness, anger, and other primary emotions in your early years.

Think about what you do with your forehead. Right now, do as many contortions with it that you can, starting with the basics:

- Brows straight up.
- Brows down hard.
- One brow arched.
- Brows knit together in the center.

Look at yourself in the mirror. How many variations can you manage with those muscles? There is an odd configuration that Greg can do that involves bringing the brows together while lifting them and jamming the wrinkles in his forehead together. He can control the grief muscle that arcs at the top. Depending on what he's doing with his mouth, he either looks a deranged killer or a deranged clown.

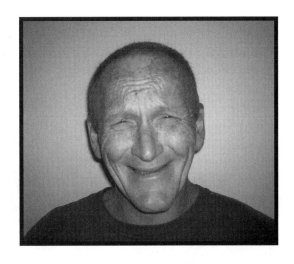

The brow is one of the most expressive speakers in all non-verbal communication.

As an exercise, put down this book and watch television news, with the sound off, for a few minutes. Take a childlike approach: Look at what's on the screen as if you don't know what to expect. Do you get the sense that these people are telegraphing what is in their head across the well-lit billboard that is the brow?

One movement you will probably notice more than others is the way people use the brow and forehead to emphasize a point or to illustrate what they mean. You can shake a hand or finger or your eyebrows or your whole head to drive home your message. Bill O'Reilly on Fox News often relies on his eyebrows as an illustrator; every day he gives life to the cliché "brow beating."

Wrinkled Forehead

Common reasons to wrinkle the brow include **surprise**, **fear**, or some form of **concern for another**, such as sympathy. The standard ways to express each are:

- Surprise is a straight up lift.
- Fear is a lift that engages an area that the French call the "grief muscle," which is the combination of those two straight lines and the arch at the top. We will refer to the grief muscle and this set of straight up and down muscles collectively as "pain muscles," because you use it both when you express pain and when you want

 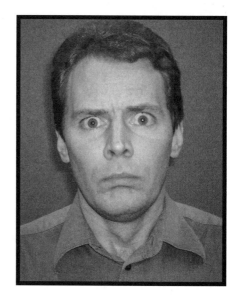

to inflict it. Someone under very high stress will often massage the pain muscle set between the eyes. This is often involuntary and an adaptor for high stress. How many times have you done it when you screwed up a project or your 13-year-old son came home and announced, "I punched a kid at school?"

This is the same gesture that people with tension headaches commonly use. It's an involuntary response to the tightening of the muscles in that area, and an unconscious attempt to stretch them and increase blood flow to the area.

- Concern also involves a straight-up lift and use of the pain muscle, but the eyes are engaged very differently. The eyes show sympathy. (More on that in the discussion of pupil dilation and contraction.)

The absence of a wrinkled brow sends certain messages as well, and two primary ones are calculated deception and Botox injections.

Eyebrows

Brow movement is so integral to human communication that actors get this element of body language right more often than any other part. Does that mean they have talent? Not as much as humanness. Brow movement may be the most inborn trait of human communication.

Eyebrow Flash or Lift

Eyebrow flash is a fleeting expression with a lifting of the brows as its primary component. This may be instant and disappear quickly. Your eyebrows flash when you **recognize someone**. It's an involuntary and universal response. During his career as a U.S. Army interrogator, Greg saw it in bringing two prisoners together who had asserted that they did not know each other. However, as soon as they saw each other, the eyebrows went up a little and he knew they were lying.

The lack of an eyebrow flash triggers your intuition that someone who should recognize you does not. The next time you see someone you know, pay attention to your brow and his. You are mirroring that person—an acknowledgment—even though you aren't conscious of your expectation for that response. When you don't get it, an awkward moment follows. A typical occasion would be your 20-year class reunion. You see someone who used to be the head cheerleader, who looks basically the same as she did in high school. You, on the other hand, have become a marathon runner—a far cry from the pudgy geek who ruled in chemistry class. Your eyebrows flash when she approaches, but she looks straight at you with no sign of ever having seen you before. And she doesn't know body language well enough to fake it.

Compound the eyebrow flash of recognition with a wrinkled brow and here's what you get: I know you, but I'm concerned about where/why/how. Here's how that might show up: A woman is at a party with her husband. They both say "hello" to a man that the husband knew very well professionally, but didn't think she knew. She did know him, though, from parties in years past—before she met her husband. The husband's colleague gives an eyebrow flash followed by a knit brow: He clearly recognizes them both, but has some concern about seeing them together. The man is concerned about what incriminating stories she might pass along.

Your brows also might flash when you **recognize an idea**, as in, "I know what you mean." Similarly, they will jut up as a way of asking the person you're with if she recognizes your idea. It's your body's way of inquiring, "Catch that?"

Eyebrows in "Request for Approval"

If the eyebrow flash is a snippet of body language, then **request for approval** is its pregnant cousin. Just as in a "catch that" moment, the person is asking whether or not you notice what he is saying. More importantly, with the request for approval he is asking *how* you perceive what he is saying. When someone is unsure of where he stands, whether he is believed, or how an action is accepted, you will commonly see the eyebrows raise and pause—even if momentarily.

The amount of time is an eternity in terms of facial expression. You see it on a regular basis and even do it yourself when you desperately want approval, but until you can identify it as a discrete gesture, you can only do it and respond instinctively, not cognitively. It is the brow version of raising the shoulders into a shrugging motion as a sign of helplessness.

Watch politicians face reporters about touchy issues, or stars field questions about a recent movie. You will see request for approval. Kids do it when they attempt something and aren't sure if they got it right, such as tossing a baseball or tying their shoes. Your wife may do it when she comes out of the bedroom with a new dress on. Your husband will do it when he presents you with a box of chocolates for Valentine's Day—a day late. Your new employee will do it when he hands you his first sales report.

Probably the most robust display of the request-for-approval expression that people in the United States have seen recently was on the campaign trail during the run-up to the 2016 presidential election. During the debates among the many Republicans, we saw all the candidates with the exception of Carly Fiorina and Donald Trump use it. The candidates would make a point that they suspected did not have overwhelming support from the audience and then, as if inviting the audience to respond favorably, would raise their eyebrows in a request for approval. The reasons Fiorina and Trump are the exception is that she appears to have an immovable forehead (think Botox) and he does not request other people's approval. We will address requests for approval in other places as well. The eyebrows are simply the first place we see these requests.

Arching an Eyebrow

Some brow movements become associated with cultural norms, such as *Star Trek's* Mr. Spock raising an eyebrow sharply as he said, "Interesting, Captain." If your mother did a version of this, looking askance at the same time to indicate displeasure, that is her norm, not necessarily a cultural norm. She may, in fact, have picked it up from her mother or the late Leonard Nimoy. Between a mother and child, that expression transmits a specific meaning, whereas the Spock-like raised eyebrow carries a more general message, which is, "Interesting." Regardless of your mother's meaning, if a person combines this raised brow with a jaundiced eye and a slight smirk, you can bet you have a credibility problem with her.

Lots of people haven't developed the muscle control to arch a single eyebrow, and few people can arch both brows separately. One of the few exceptions is our model in this section, Kurtis Kelly. Since Kurtis is an actor, this could be a matter of practice, but then again, there's seems to be a correlation between handedness and which eyebrow a person typically raises. Incidentally, Kurtis appears to be ambidextrous in many things.

Try it: Raise one eyebrow. Is it your left? Then you're probably right handed.

Brow and Eyes in Orchestration

You can send a very clear message with a pair of glasses. Raise your brow and look over your glasses. If you're 16, it's funny. If you're 46, it's **condescending and pushy**. It's an authoritarian look. Looking across the bridge of your nose, even without the glasses, delivers the same effect. If your face is structured correctly it is a very predatory look; at any rate the look is one of condemnation.

Take the opposite approach: Tilt your head back and look over your cheekbones without a facial expression at someone. What does this convey? The language is universal, but in English, the description has even become a cliché: looking down your nose at someone. The message of the gesture is so clear that it can effectively be used as a regulator to control conversation.

Absolute Brow Control

Brows punctuate our messages. If you were capable of absolute brow control, the impact on your communication style would make you surreal. It could also make you a potentially excellent screen actor like Kevin Spacey, who has demonstrated throughout his career—from *The Usual Suspects* (in 1995) to *House of Cards* (currently in its fifth season in 2016)—that brow control can plant sympathy or fear in the heart of the person who sees it.

As Roger (Verbal) Kint in the classic thriller *The Usual Suspects*, which has made a lot of "best movies of all time" lists, Spacey calmly participates in an interrogation with an obvious *lack* of body language from his brows. Kint refers to himself as a CP (Cerebral Palsy), and exhibits signs of both debilitation and mental impairment, so his oddly still face projects a subhuman quality. (Note: This discussion is necessarily a spoiler, so if you haven't seen the movie, watch it and then come back to this section.) When U.S. Customs agent Dave Kujan (Chazz Palminteri) drops a bombshell, however, Kint shows use of the pain muscle that seems to punctuate genuine surprise at the revelation. (Is the surprise the information itself, or the fact that Kujan has it?) Later in the movie, when Kujan mentions the name of the notorious criminal, Keyser Söze, Kint explodes. Described in various terms as the devil incarnate, Keyser Söze is a powerful force whose very name agitates those who know of him. The logical conclusion from the outburst (one that most law enforcement officers and audience members would draw) is that shock produces involuntary and universal responses; in other words, honest responses. When that happens, many parts of the face reveal the surprise, but particularly the brow. As a corollary, one might conclude that Kint is a dullard who doesn't have the capacity to express feelings normally (hence the lack of brow movement) or he just mimics his prison buddies who stay cool under pressure, but regardless of which scenario is true, ballistic Kint seems like the real deal.

The interrogation proceeds. As Kint seems to develop a sense of comfort, or at least familiarity with Kujan, he begins to tell stories with an animated face. Here is where a serious student of body language gets suspicious: The baseline for him indicates his normal expression was non-expression, so he seems deceitful when he uses his brow in a typically "normal" way. Spacey's Kint soon appears to uncoil, losing his control as he talks about the shoot-out, expressing grief over the loss of his friend; there's lot of brow action here. He even makes a disarming statement to Kujan that the reason he didn't run away was that he was afraid—and he accents it perfectly with raised eyebrows, the standard indication of "request for approval."

At the end, we find out just how good an actor the character Kint is. If there is any screen character who seems to support Desmond Morris's theory about a human being's control over facial muscles, it would be Kint. We are not dealing with a real human being in Kint; we're seeing the output of a gifted actor, Kevin Spacey. He's the mastermind behind the brows that tell nothing and tell everything. Control over the brow, an usually uncontrollable part of the face, is Spacey's stock-in-trade, an integral part of his talent. He acts from the brows down until the scene demands a show of emotion, and then he punctuates it with the appropriate brow movement.

Contrast this with the android Data of *Star Trek: The Next Generation*. Poor Data longs to be human, but cannot feel emotion. Eyebrows, corner of the mouth, eyes—everything moves on Data's "emotionless" face. In fact, put him with Captain Picard and Lieutenant Worf, and his face will likely be the most animated.

Some animated films have done a superlative job of using eyebrow movement to punctuate messages and clarify emotions of a character. The animators have the ability to impose absolute control, of course. A great example is *Inside Out* (2015), an animated film that features characters who embody a 12-year-old girl's key emotions. In it, the Pixar geniuses used eyebrow movement that reinforced our perception of the emotions portrayed by the characters called Joy, Fear, Anger, Disgust, and Sadness.

Eyes

A 16th-century proverb calls the eyes "the windows to the soul." More than 500 years later, the proverb has assumed the stature of gospel. When you really understand the eyes, you'll see how the close the proverb is to the mark.

Temples

Moving down the face, we come to areas that surface a lot of involuntary and universal body language: the eyes and areas along the edges of the eyes. In the 19th century, French physician Guillaume Duchenne studied the physiology of the smile. He learned that two primary muscles drive a real smile: the zygomatic major (that raise the corners of the mouth) and the orbicularis oculi (that control the cheeks and produce crow's feet around the eyes). A genuine smile that engages both of these muscle sets is referred to as the Duchenne smile even today.

When you fake a smile, the muscles responsible for the temple area, the orbicularis oculi, do not move. When you smile up to your eyes—**a real smile**—they crinkle. Only a very small percentage of the population can affect that kind of smile and not mean it.

A baby's smile offers the most genuine vision of happiness on the planet. Nothing is filtered. Nothing is faked. The photo on this page shows Delaney Skye Ott-Dahl, daughter of Keston and Andrea Ott-Dahl, who is the "star" of the book written by her parents, *Saving Delaney* (Cleis, 2016).

Pupils

Pupils dilate naturally in constant light for a few reasons (among many): attraction, fear, and interest. When a human sees **something attractive sexually,** the eyes dilate to get as much of a good thing as possible. Watch the eyes of a heterosexual teenage boy getting his first look at a naked woman.

In the peripheral nervous system, the sympathetic prepares us for fight-or-flight. The parasympathetic is a braking mechanism that calms and places us in an un-aroused state. The arousal can be anytime we are in a new situation or a situation perceived as a threat. One of the results of the sympathetic kicking in is that the pupils dilate to take in more data about the threat.

In a normal state of arousal, human pupils are neither dilated nor pinpointed; they are somewhere in between. Pinpointed pupils usually indicate that a person does not like what he is looking at, and it can be part of the complex facial actions that signal rage.

Eye Movement

Eye movement signals you are **looking for answers inside your head.** It's a phenomenon generally associated with neuro-linguistic programming (NLP), which asserts that automatic eye movements often correspond to particular thought processes. But NLP is a product of the 1970s, whereas medical literature addresses "visual accessing cues" in the late 19th century. In the 1890 book *Principles of Psychology*, the "Father of American psychology" William James said:

> I cannot think in visual terms without feeling a fluctuating play of pressures, convergences, divergences, and accommodations in my eyeballs.... When I try to remember or reflect, the movements in question...feel like a sort of withdrawal from the outer world. As far as I can detect, these feelings are due to an actual rolling outwards and upwards of the eyeballs.[1]

The visual cortex is at the back of the brain, so in recalling an image your eyes will likely drift upward. When we say "upward" in regards to visual accessing we mean above the brow ridge. The portions of your brain that process sound are located directly over the ears, so in recalling a melody or noise, your eyes tend to drift toward your ears usually between the brow ridge and cheek bone. Cognitive thought and problem-solving occur in the frontal lobe in adults. When calculating or analyzing, you will find your eyes—and perhaps your whole head—moving down left. A down-right movement corresponds to intense feelings.

Using questions that target specific sensory channels and specific parts of the brain—visual, auditory, and cognitive—you can drive another person to move his eyes. Watch what happens when you pose the following questions to someone or answer the questions yourself:

- What did your first-grade classroom look like?
- What is the 10th word of "The Star Spangled Banner"?
- What is 30 percent of $54?
- What do you think the inside of the Voyager Space Probes looks like?
- What kind of sound does a giraffe make?
- What did you feel when you heard about the deaths of innocents and heroes on 9/11?

This exercise demonstrates that eye movement is natural and linked to brain structures. When someone recalls information from the memory side of the visual cortex, that is visual memory. Visual construct is occurring when the person's eyes move up, but to the side opposite the memory side. Knowing which side is which for an individual helps you develop a baseline, so when you ask him a question you'll know if he's remembering or creating. You can use the same principle to determine whether someone is remembering a sound or creating one. Finally, except for Basques, who don't seem to fit standard patterns of eye movement, you will see a person who is computing or considering a problem look down-left, and someone overcome by emotion looking down-right.

Maryann attended a final chapel service at a camp near her. Six campers took turns giving short speeches on "what camp means to me." The last speaker, a girl who had just completed her final season at camp, got choked up as she recalled seven seasons of camp experiences. Maryann noticed that the heads of about a hundred people on the benches in front of her tilted slightly to the right during the emotional speech.

Eyelids

A woman who wears eye makeup every day could easily spend $250 a year on her eyelids alone. Add to that the cost of blepharoplasty, a common procedure to remove fat deposits, excess tissue, and muscle from the eyelids. The American Academy of Facial Plastic and Reconstructive Surgery says 100,000 men and women in the United States have it every year at an average cost of $2,500 for the upper eyelids and $3,000 for the lower. In short, it is possible for a person to spend tens of thousands of dollars in his or her lifetime on those tiny bits of flesh known as eyelids. They must be pretty important.

The makeup and plastic surgery contribute to the passive messages that eyelids convey, primarily, "I'm young(ish). I'm vibrant. I'm sexy." Excess skin around the eyes, even when it occurs in a juvenile, has an aging effect. It makes a person look less awake and more matronly. People with naturally baggy eyes look tired, or even sad. They don't photograph well, and when they realize that, they may go out of their way to stand behind grandpa in family photos. Sagging upper lids and puffy lower lids can contribute to some very self-conscious body language, particularly in men and women who spent their youth enjoying the adulation of the opposite sex because of their facial beauty.

An eye twitch signals **stress** unless it's associated with neurological damage. The only way to tell is to observe the person in a completely relaxed state.

An eyelid droop means the person feels intense stress. This is the kind of reaction a prisoner of war or a person held at gunpoint might have, or a U.S. president after years in office, because they all show this sign. In addition to stress causing a droop in the lower lid, stress engages the sympathetic nervous system, which draws blood from the mucosa and redirects it to the muscles for a fight-or-flight response. The lack of blood causes the lower eyelid to sag in addition to other responses, such as a thinning of the lips.

A much more common sight is that of a child just beginning to understand the concept of object permanence. You see him closing his eyes to make you disappear. Many children, when first discovering this, will think that closing his or her eyes means you can't see him or her, either. Lids can be used by adults in similar fashion, such as closing the eyes to prevent seeing something that does not mesh with what they are trying to portray. It helps maintain stability and prevent displaced expectations. Similarly, averting the eyes is not uncommon. We see this in people who do not know how to deal with people with disabilities. The more sophisticated version comes when someone knows you can read eyes, and closes their eyes as a solid barrier against discovery.

In deliberately using eyelids, a person might also do one of the following:

- Close the lids partially as a barrier to further conversation or contact.
- Squeeze one eyelid shut as part of expressing extreme disbelief.
- Wink as a way to flirt, as a sign of "okay" or "I understand," or as a request for approval, depending on what the rest of the face is doing.
- Squeeze both eyelids shut to express emotional or physical pain, or profound concentration.
- Squint the eyes at the subject to express condemnation or judgment.

Blink Rate

Everyone has a normal blink rate, which is his baseline. When you ask questions that are not stress-inducing, the rate is constant. When the stress increases, whether from emotional stimulus or a person's fear of discovery that he is lying or bluffing, the blink rate may increase exponentially. It's possible to see a three-to-fourfold increase when a person is trying to lie.

Ears

Ears often flush when people are **worried about being discovered**—that is, afraid of being embarrassed, as opposed to already being embarrassed. Some people's ears will blush when they're **bluffing** as well, so watch for that at the poker table.

We might involuntarily send signals by touching our ears too. As adults, many of us occasionally revert back to the childhood way of blocking out something we don't want to hear by muting the sound. However, instead of slamming our palms against our ears and screaming we'll probably rest our head on our hand or brush the ears with our fingertips while someone is talking as a symbolic gesture to turn down the volume. People may even do this when they are talking about something that is unpleasant to their own ears, such as a lie. Similar to many adult behaviors, this is an echo of something that has worked in our past.

Pulling the ear or lightly rubbing the ear are both common movements, but they don't send any particular message by themselves—unless you're Carol Burnett. She used to tug on her ear at the end of each show to let her grandmother know she was okay. Rubbing or pulling an ear could be just space fillers for a person, indicating "I'm thinking" or "I'm bored." You'll need other indicators to conclude that this means the person is nervous (for example, flushed ears or eyes reaching hard to the construct side of the brain while the action occurs).

For some people, ears are an erogenous zone, so you should look at how the person touches his or her ear. Is it a delicate touch? Rough rubbing? A little scratch? Self-stroking the ear is one of many adapters that involve touching the skin to provide comfort. Or in the case of Maryann's cat, sometimes it's just an itchy ear.

Nose

It's amazing how many vessels are in the nose—a phenomenon that is especially obvious in the touring exhibits featuring human bodies that have been subjected to plastination. This technique sucks moisture from cadavers and then coats and fills them with plastic. It preserves the bodies so that they can be placed into static positions so that viewers can examine musculature, nerves, the circulatory system, and so on. It allows for a unique view of organs and other body parts that have been sliced similar to onions. A plastinated nose shows so many blood vessels that it appears to be one solid mass.

Developmental researcher Kang Lee has developed an image processing technology that non-invasively takes researchers "underneath the skin" to show the massive number of blood vessels in the nose and rest of the face. Lee sees evidence underneath the skin of what we have been telling readers about in our books on body language and lie detection: A person has natural stress responses to lying. These responses may be undetectable to the untrained eye, and may even be undetectable to the trained eye, but they are there. Lee's optical imaging technology, which has an effectiveness rate of about 85 percent in detecting lies, is designed to document those responses by focusing on changes in facial blood flow. The nose, therefore, is the most sensitive part of the body, due in large part to its vascularity.[2]

A person **under stress** will commonly touch her nose, whether it's a light scratch or rub. Just touching the nose doesn't signal stress, however. Sometimes touching the nose means a person is **disgusted** with something. The whole gesture will be different from a stress gesture, however. It could be a wipe with the back of a hand (when there's no reason to wipe), or a finger joint against the nose, as if to block something stinky from making its way inside.

As opposed to what many people think (one indicator of this is how many journalists have asked me to affirm this in interviews) you cannot tell whether or not a person is lying just because he's scratching his nose. However, if he's doing excessive nose handling then you can tell something is going on in his head because he's probably responding to increased vascular action.

Wrinkling the nose in intentional communication is almost always a female gesture. Many men cannot even seem to do it. The exception is the involuntary wrinkling of the nose signaling disgust.

Mouth

Take a look at any magazine with fashion models and you will see many with their mouths slightly open. It's probably an attempt to project sexy and vulnerable, but this mouth position is often part of the "stupid look"—the look of mouth breathers. When the model combines it with a blank stare, she looks brain dead. So, if the object is to get across that she's no threat, the photographer certainly succeeded. Note: None of the male models have this look.

When done in combination with a wrinkled brow, a crinkle to the nose and pulling the corners of the mouth down signals disgust, one of the seven identifiable facial expressions that we consider among the few "absolutes" of body language. (We go more in depth about this in Chapter 4.)

Covering the mouth is a simple barrier loaded with meaning. It could mean so many things that this gesture provides a great example of the importance of context. Why would anyone cover his or her mouth?

- Trying to eat and talk at the same time, which is a gesture hugely impacted by culture.
- Self-conscious about her teeth.
- Shy; unwilling to smile broadly because it's uncomfortable.
- Doesn't want you to hear what she's saying and this is a barrier thrown up subconsciously to mute the sound.

Although we explore combinations of moves later in the book, let's start moving into the topic here. If a person is self-conscious about her teeth, she'll first signal that by drawing her lips down over her teeth, smiling with lips together. Notice that this close-lipped smile may even engage the muscles at the corner of her eyes. That means it's a genuine smile, and it is not an indication of bad feelings or deceit just because she doesn't show her teeth. That smile can offer just as much, or more, warmth as the toothiest grin.

When a person's mind is completely engaged, he may unconsciously do things with his mouth that are odd, and almost abusive. Chewing on the inside of the mouth, licking the lips repeatedly, sticking the tongue out, biting a lip, biting chapped skin on the lip (maybe even causing bleeding), and twisting the mouth to the side are among common movements. What his eyes are doing give away more of the story. Look for signs of emotion (down-right), calculation (down-left), and so on.

Another completely involuntary move that a mouth will make is the quiver resulting from being startled. It's an uncontrollable movement—a purely stimulus-response gesture. Would any human respond the same way to a sudden noise or dropping something, for example? No, and the reasons are varied. Someone less sensitive to noise might not react that way. Someone who doesn't care about having dropped something might not react that way. Elements of body language come together to create a message through signaling, so each separate signal does not have an absolute meaning. Take the simple raising of the brow that shows surprise, add to it a crinkle of the brow and a downturn the mouth, and you now have the emotion of fear. The point is simple: This is an orchestra you are reading, not a drum solo.

Lips

Another movement that also involves the mouth is licking the lips. Children lick their lips when they're thinking. So do horses, as well as a lot of adults. It's one sign that the **brain is engaged**. Lip biting can also signal thinking, but suggests a more stressful topic.

Men will sometimes purse and grip their lips so their lips almost disappear. Often, that is a man holding **back emotion**. In the video of Lyndon Johnson at the Democratic National Convention that chose John F. Kennedy over him to be the presidential candidate, he leaks frustration, annoyance, and even anger when he's faced with the "opportunity" to be vice president. His lips assume a sucked-in grimace, and he tilts his head down during speaking. Even though the words coming out of his mouth are conciliatory "...my friend, John F. Kennedy...," his body language says that he was choking back emotion. Look at the 2016 image of Bernie Sanders and Hillary Clinton as Sanders endorsed Clinton. His oversized toothy smile is replaced with lip grip even if combined with a smile. Look for images of any of the American presidents, and probably other heads of state as well, and you will see the lip grip during moments of heightened emotion. It took us less than five minutes to come up with spot-on images of Presidents Bill Clinton, George Bush, and Barack Obama doing lip grips—and, of course, each faced crises during their administrations.

Fight-or-flight has an impact on the lips as well. When the sympathetic nervous system kicks in, it gives blood to things needed for fight-or-flight, such as muscles, the lungs, and the heart. It takes blood away from "useless" things such as the highly evolved primate brain and the reproductive and digestive systems. A direct result is blood leaving all mucosa. This means the lips become drawn and thin.

Unlike fight-or-flight demands, the mucous membranes need more blood flow in times of sexual arousal. Because the body requires high blood flow for erections, sensitivity, and lubrication, the body floods mucosa with blood. The result is red cheeks and full lips. We can see it in both men and women. It is the reason that the Angelina Jolie "pillow lip" has become so admired. It is a sign of attraction in a woman, and easy for even the least perceptive of men to recognize as a flirtatious look.

Smile

Another facial sign, but one that varies from person to person, is the smile. Here is the difference between a practiced, perfect C-shaped smile and a smile that rises to the eyes: One is for presentation. And one is genuine.

Take a look at people you know well and notice the difference between their relaxed smile and the one they use as part of establishing control. Remember: A smile that doesn't reach the eyes broadcasts insincerity; the person doesn't look happy even if a grin is present.

Consider the possible origins of a human smile. So many animals bare their teeth in something that might be described as a smile. In a chimp, a smile means fear. Did our human smiles develop as a way of making ourselves less threatening to other chimps? Perhaps our ancestors found the smile a quick way of alerting another chimp that they had no intention of causing harm. They chose to express fear so they would not be perceived as a threat. Both chimps would put their guard down and everyone remained alive.

In the first year of their lives, when baby horses walk up to adult horses they will do something that we might call a smile. Once again, however, it's the fear expression that communicates to adults, "I'm weaker than you. Don't hurt me."

A few of the common smiles that communicate a distinct message are:

- When former President George W. Bush said something and wanted to know whether or not his audience would approve of it, he made a goofy, country-boy smile. You could tell when he was uncertain about how people would perceive him.
- Former President Barack Obama engaged his whole face, full-tooth smile when he was about to launch a well-prepared assault on an opponent or when genuinely pleased. The difference is the orbicularis oculi. One looks aggressive, the other welcoming.
- Movie stars on the red carpet often use a camera smile. It's even, with teeth showing, and no engagement of the orbicularis oculi muscles around the eyes. This is a polite, public smile.
- The amused smile is one you see among audience members at the Ellen deGeneres show when someone on stage says something mildly humorous. It engages the temple muscles, but exposure of teeth is limited or non-existent. The brain is amused and the smiler is not trying to send a message.
- For an example of the seductive smile, think Eva Green as Vesper Lynd in the remake of the James Bond film *Casino Royale*—playful eyes and a tilt of the head.

- A smile of recognition shows genuine happiness if you like the person and simple politeness if you do not. Regardless of the form it takes, it always involves the involuntary eyebrow flash associated with recognizing someone.

- A smile of discomfort often appears on the face of the spouse being dragged to a 20th high school class reunion, or on the face of a shy 13-year-old boy who's meeting the new, pretty girl at school. It's a tight-lipped smile that might be accompanied by the request-for-approval.

Jaw

A stern jaw typically conveys masculinity or anger, as opposed to a slack jaw, which sends the message of "I am non-threatening—and I'm stupid."

It's hard to look stern when you don't have a chin. The jaw is a powerful symbol. Combine the male set jaw with brows drawn together in anger and beady eyes and you have the picture of someone who looks intimidating. It's the core segment of a body-language picture designed to instill fear. Now consider how different this jaw is on a woman's face. It can be comical, as comedians such as Carol Burnett and her Tarzan howling, and Debra Messing and her bulldog scowling have shown. Men, too, have taken advantage of the comic possibilities of the large jaw and the fact that it enables the kind of rubbery facial expressions of Jim Carrey.

Contrast the big-mouthed, full-jawed look of some women such as Julia Roberts with the pouty-mouthed picture of Bernadette Peters. Julia Roberts can play the range of emotions from silly to sorrowful to nasty, partly because her facial structure supports that range. Can Peters ever look fierce? She can sound vicious, but that little mouth of hers opens and we still see cute—despite the fact that her talent is expansive. Let's envision her in as a heinous criminal. Combine that angelic mouth with an expressionless brow as she tells you how she is going to kill you. The result is surreal and disturbing because it fits none of our preconceived notions.

Head and Neck

Head tilts often correspond with the eye movement previously described. For example, the down-right look of someone in a state of deep emotion may also involve the entire head plunging down-right, which is a posture you will see at funerals. Head tilts or bobs may also serve to reinforce a statement or substitute for it. The sharply cocked head indicating, "You don't really mean that" needs no words behind it. And a head moving similar to a bobble-head doll, at least in the American culture, suggests uncertainty.

One example of that was when disgraced Tour de France cyclist Floyd Landis and his (now former) wife were on the *Today* show. Amber Landis moved her head back and forth like a bobble-head doll when Matt Lauer asked her if she believed her husband's claim of innocence. Her voice said "Yes," but her head said "I don't know." Another variation of the head and neck disconnecting from what's coming out of the mouth is a "no" movement side to side—again, common in the United States, but not all cultures—when the person is saying "yes" (or vice versa). During the 2016 U.S. presidential campaign one blogger who focused on lie detection wrote:

On a 2016 episode of *60 Minutes*, Secretary of State Hillary Clinton was asked about the animosity between her and President Barack Obama during the Democratic Primary campaign.

"And you've repaired all of that [ill-will]?" CBS journalist Scott Pelley asked the Secretary of State.

"Oh, of course. Yes," Clinton said. "We have a great relationship!"

But as she uttered those words, her face told a different story. While saying "Yes," Clinton shook her head side-to-side as if she had answered the question "No."[3]

Another type of head tilt is the raised chin, typically done deliberately to express indignation. Take notice how often this occurs in interview/talk shows. When asked a personal question, the guest might raise her chin as an involuntary way of gesturing "I don't have to answer that."

When Senator Ted Cruz walked onto the Republican National Convention stage to deliver his speech he walked out with a chin held uncharacteristically high in the 2016 debates. Cruz delivered his speech without endorsing Trump and walked off stage. Greg commented on the chin-up entrance as unusual for Cruz as he walked on stage. It was a sign that suggested a robust endorsement of Trump was not forthcoming.

The neck has throbbing veins and arteries that can indicate temporary stress or a chronic condition such as hypertension. Rubbing the neck is an instinctive reaction to discomfort that can be associated with distended veins, or just a sense that the neck is warm and a cool hand on it would feel good. Every touch does not convey information about someone's emotional state. Sometimes an itch is just an itch.

Limbs

Shoulders

One surprising result from our TV watching related to this book was observing male actors. More than one tended to display anger with rounded shoulders, a jaw that was tucked down, and open hands. We have news for you, tough guys: This is the body language of an angry woman.

Shoulders back on a man or woman conveys **control and alertness**, which is why everyone in the U.S. military either stands that way when called to attention or faces the prospect of a weekend learning how to do it right. And unlike the actors we watched, men will throw their shoulders back and flare their upper back muscles (if they know how), as a sign of **power**, with or without anger.

Arms

In the discussion of categories of signals that follows this section, you will see how much we use our arms as a means to punctuate points made verbally, as well as to let other people know what they should or should not be doing. We flail, point elbows, and use them similar to how a conductor uses a baton. We move them forward to shut people out and open them to let people in. Most of the combination signals we will explore later involve the face and arms.

In any analysis of the meaning of limb movement, the first three things to consider are height, culture, and build. In baselining someone to read their body language, these must be part of the picture or your conclusions could be way off.

- Man who gestures with his hands low: British, Germanic descended.
- Man who gestures with his hands high: Mediterranean, Latin (or Bernie Sanders).

Mediterranean and Latin people have a full-bodied approach to conversation, with the hands moving at face level. Germanic people have a natural tendency to gesticulate with the hands below shoulder level, although media trainers sometimes succeed in getting their executive and political clients to gesticulate higher for the cameras. If you were an actor tasked with portraying an old British man, what is one thing you might not do? Old Anglo men commonly don't raise their elbows above their waist.

The best illustration of why we baseline is Bernie Sanders, the poster child for being an "old white guy" in dress and speech. Look at his orangutan signaling and you will realize culture is only part of the equation; this is why you need a baseline for each individual.

Now, examine the differences between effeminate gay and straight. Why does Cameron Tucker in *Modern Family* look so much gayer than his husband Mitchell Pritchett? Watch how he moves his arms—how high they are—as compared to Mitchell the lawyer who has less flagrant displays of passion. Mitchell looks more masculine, even doing the same family of gestures, because his movements are generally lower.

Legs

Greg is tall with relatively thick legs, so he generally sits either with his legs in a "V" or with one foot slung over the opposite leg. A few years ago, he was doing an interview with *Der Spiegel* with his legs in the latter position and the reporter accused him of being cocky. "That's not cocky, that's relaxed," he explained to her. Sitting like a "European gentleman" is uncomfortable and awkward with a build like that.

A woman can make a deliberate **power statement** by sitting with her legs crossed and her high heel pointed at someone. It is a statement about confidence through sexuality, confidence through taste in selecting that shoe, and assertiveness by aiming the heel at the person. The message: Yes, I'm a woman, but I can deal with you like a man; I have power here. It is an attempt to emasculate.

Legs can move back and forth as a result of nervous energy. You may sometimes see young men sitting with the legs moving back and forth. This is a comforting move as the thighs and genitalia make contact. Few, if any, realize they are doing it.

Hips

If a man puts his hands on his hips, it means **defiance**, as long as his fingers are pointed toward his crotch. It's an obvious symbol of masculinity.

Women typically put their hands on their hips with fingers pointed toward the butt cheeks to show the same emotion. If a man does that, some may perceive it as looking feminine. Contrast a man and a women standing arrogantly and cocky. One demonstrates masculinity by framing the genitals and the other demonstrates feminine power by pointing toward her assets in the rear. Displays of power make us exaggerate the gestures of the gender we identify with.

Extremities

Hands

Most of what is in this section on hands will be in the section on holistic expressions because a majority of meaningful hand signals involve other body parts. The fig-leaf posture is one example. Watch men of different cultures in diverse situations do it. The one thing they have in common if they feel the least bit threatened is an involuntary compulsion to, in a phrase that J.R.R. Tolkein's Golem would use, "protect the precious."

Fidgeting hands, picking at cuticles, and an autoerogenous finger rubbing are all potential signs of stress and/or attempts at stress relief and creating familiar in the unfamiliar. But again, without context, what you may be observing is nothing more than an annoying personal habit.

Grooming of the hands sends messages, too, but they may be mixed. If a police interrogator asks a suspect "What do you do?" and he replies "I'm a computer programmer," but he has calloused hands, is the suspect believable? Either the person is lying, or he does something in his spare time that tears up his hands. Good questioning gets the story behind the body language, and it can give you an edge in both business and personal relationships.

Grooming practices with hands become almost unconscious because people tend to look at their hands more than other body parts. Here's Greg's theory about this: Hands are the only tools we own from birth and as such we can't easily identify with them as part of us. They are tools. There may be no significant meaning at all associated with pushing back the cuticles during a meeting, for example. If it is a sign of anything, it probably means the person is a little bored rather than stressed. If a person without well-groomed hands tries to cover them

up in your presence, that's a sign she's **embarrassed**, or at the very least, **feels insecure** around you. Curling hands is a similar sign.

When you see someone do something bizarre with his hands, he may raise questions in our mind. If someone repeats a gesture over and over, such as a secret signal that designates you as a member of a gang, it stays with you in some form. The Army had a number of unofficial hand signals, too, such as the one

depicted in the photo on this page. In Army parlance, it meant "Cover me, I'm screwed," or in polite terms, "My weapon's jammed." One former Army guy may sneak it to another former Army guy in a business meeting and no one would know about his cry for help.

Feet

A person can have many reasons for crossing his feet; you definitely need context to know whether or not that means he is shutting you out. For starters, take his anatomy into account. A tall person in a low chair will either have his feet crossed or his knees in his ears. A woman who was raised to adopt "modest" posture will habitually cross her feet because her mother spent 18 years telling her that's how ladies sit.

Contrast with that the subconscious act of turning the toes inward, an action that reflects **subjugation**, especially in a sexual situation. Young women will often sit with their toes turned inward in sexual circumstances where they are not in charge. Something deep inside her "orders" her to adopt a submissive pose.

People in **stressful situations** will commonly point their feet toward the door. Greg has noticed this many times while interviewing management candidates for various companies.

The grooming of the feet is usually less obvious than the hands, of course, but in sandal weather or intimate situations in which someone's bare feet are near you, grooming can say a lot about issues of femininity, athleticism, and basic hygiene. Showing ugly feet in sandals may be comfortable, but you can expect some people to think less of you.

Utterances

In addition to proximity, time, movement, culture, and other essential topics in the field of body language, an important one is vocalics, or "utterances." Vocalics is an area of non-verbal communication studies because it's about how something is said rather than what is being said. "Ah," "hmmm," "ick," "ewww," "yuck," and "uh" are a few of them, and the roles they play in communication can vary:

- They change the pace of communication.
- They fill otherwise dead air, but don't necessarily tell you much. Watch eye movement, hands, tilt of the head, and so on to find out if the utterance is an expression of visualizing, disgust, confusion, creation, and so on.
- Depending on what vocal quality you pick up—strident, lyrical, coarse, breathy—you will get a sense of the person's emotions.

In reviewing body language, you will also pick up utterances that relate to tone or pronunciations that seem abnormal to you. These can be subtle aspects of speech that give away information about a person's port of origin. We don't mean a full-blown Boston accent or Georgia-boy style of talking; we are referring to the way many Northern Americans and Canadians pronounce "ou," and the way people from Pennsylvania Dutch country have a tendency to go up in pitch at the end of a sentence and down when asking a question. If you pick that up, you have an extra clue about sub-cultural influences: If the person lived in that area, or with people from that area long enough to pick up such a regionalism, then chances are good that the body language shows it, too.

The Impact of Disability

With disability comes an adaptation of human behavior in the same sense as adapting to a new culture. Communication may take on forms not considered typical by the society. Looking at it from the outside, the result may place the disabled person in a sub-typical role. Looking at it from the inside, the result may be that the disabled person wants to prove how typical or super-typical she is.

If a birth defect places the person in a life-long struggle to overcome the sub-typical role, imagine the struggle when the disability occurs in adult life through trauma or disease. Franklin Delano Roosevelt was 39 years old when polio struck and paralyzed both of his legs up to the hips. FDR fought for normalcy through rehabilitation that was both costly and difficult. How did this impact his sense of belonging and even his policies of entitlement of average Americans?

Regardless of the type of disability, physically challenged people have something in common: steps, curbs, and banks of snow present problems. Some people find unity in physical adversity; others live their lives as if it's irrelevant. As we look more closely at the holistic view of body language in Chapter 5, you will see how this manifests itself in open versus closed movements—even in cases when disability severely limits movement.

Disability can blind people on the outside to the real person and how the person's culture impacts her psyche. The natural reaction of an unaffected person is to feel guilt and remorse and to over-accommodate, which, in its own way, is treating the person as sub-typical. Activists such as Marta Russell criticized Mother Teresa for building a homeless shelter in New York City without elevators to accommodate the disabled. She responded that an elevator is a luxury that would cost soup and sandwiches. We could extrapolate to say that Mother Teresa concluded that the needs of a great number of sub-typical people—the homeless in New York—surpassed the needs of a minority, who may not be sub-typical at all. (And are we to think that the good sisters wouldn't walk downstairs to give a sandwich to a homeless man in a wheelchair?)

Body Adornments

Body language encompasses both voluntary and involuntary movements, but you should not stop there. In some cases, hair, clothing, accessories, and body art can clarify the message, or are an integral part of it. In others, they distract from the meaning. Consider the case of the Toronto police officer who got away with murder for 30 years. Finally convicted in 1999 with the help of DNA evidence, Ron West had shot and killed two women with young children at home. They saw him at the door and let him in. Any suspicion they might have gleaned from his body language no doubt faded because his police uniform projected trust and protection.

As we mentioned previously, iconic elements of a costume—in this case a badge and other accoutrements of law enforcement—conveyed a specific message. Knowing this on some level, most people consciously choose their appearance. It may relate to lifestyle and occupation, but within the limits of those, we usually still have some range about hairstyles, clothes, and body art. They are an outcrop of how we want people to perceive us, and how we fit in our culture.

In learning to R.E.A.D., therefore, you will learn the relative importance of what is on the body as well as what it does. As with body parts, we'll start with the scalp and quickly work down to the toes in looking at body adornments.

Hairstyles offer great insights into intent. Stylists will readily admit that people come in often and ask for a hairstyle that is impossible to deliver. She wants a sleek upsweep for her wedding even though she has kinky hair, or a mohawk even though he has a receding hairline and bald spots. The customers get mad at the stylists because if they want a particular look, the stylist should be able to create it. They want to send a message; they insist on it, whether or not it makes sense.

Hats can have a simple, utilitarian function or have a definite message projection. What conclusions do you draw when you see a cowboy hat on someone who's not a cowboy, a baseball hat on backward, or a hat that goes perfectly with an outfit?

This comfort factor—having the outside match the image of oneself on the inside—is why a woman might develop a "relationship" with a designer, whether she's investing in haute couture or buying off the rack. She feels that the designer understands her personality as well as functional requirements related to the garment. Oleg Cassini designed more than 300 outfits as the personal couturier for Jacqueline Kennedy during her days as First Lady. His clothes framed her charisma. Even a young woman with less money than a Kennedy will clearly reveal something about her personality by choosing Stella McCartney over Laura Ashley.

Part of this experience is tribal, too. It is human nature to want to express identity through a "look" and to enhance a sense of belonging through dress. Clothing choices matter in order to develop confidence for the wearer and to influence the message received by others.

There are plenty of people who are, as Southerners might say, "too poor to paint, too proud to whitewash." (For Northern readers, that phrase is applied to old-money Southerners who do not have any old or new money, but they still have the house. They don't want anyone to know they don't have any money, though, so they let the fence rot rather than spruce it up with lime and water.) A woman in this category might identify herself through a "classic" look, even though she would look a lot more presentable if she put the moth-eaten "classics" back in the steamer trunk and spent $100 at Wal-Mart. But to her, "new" equals "bad."

Watches and pens are extensions of body language, too. If you have an expensive watch, and you aren't on the *Forbes* 100 list, you might use gestures and wear shirts and jackets that allow you show off that $10,000 Rolex—even though you never look at it because your iPhone is your main timepiece.

You can tell if someone is stuck in a period through elements similar to these examples as well. For instance, flower children wearing organic cotton skirts still live in Berkeley, California, although instead of being 20-something babes, they're now 70-something grandmothers.

Finally, "why every shoe tells a story" is not only a question to be answered here, but it is one tackled in *National Geographic* by Senior Writer Cathy Newman. She quotes both designers and historians in unequivocally pointing to the effect of shoes on body language, the statements that shoes make about social status, and the roles shoes play in projecting intent.[4] Among the most salient points are:

- The blatant sexual body language that very high heels force: breasts out, butt out, and the perception of a longer leg.

- Conveying wealth by having the soles of a shoe—or in the case of the Sioux, a moccasin—dirt-free. The Sioux used their clean, beaded moccasins as signs that they could afford to ride horses rather than walk.

- Expressing an attitude. Newman describes some of the made-to-order shoes in Olga Berluti's Warrior collection, priced at $4,000 to $12,000 a pair, as "shoes with the sleek, managing profile of a mako shark, shoes decorated with piercings, tattoos, sometimes scars…shoes for the hidden warrior inside every man."

- Allowing the style to have a transformative effect. This is the story of the woman who wears sensible heels to the office, and then comes home and replaces them with stiletto-heeled, thigh-high boots.

You don't even have to polish the soles of your shoes, as former *Vogue* editor Diana Vreeland reportedly did to be "well-heeled," which is a phrase that really means something in our culture. Someone with worn, unpolished shoes translates into "poor," or at least "careless," throughout the country. As a former soldier, "well-heeled" takes on another meaning for Greg. Anyone who spends hours every day running and hiking in boots understands that they are the most important part of your outfit. Your feet are everything.

Contrast that with this argument: Sacrificing comfort for style can be so psychologically rewarding that the mental pain of wearing "good" shoes (that is, good for foot health) is devastating. The psychological comfort is more important than the physical comfort. A pointy-toed Manolo Blahnik may indeed, as Newman says, be a "corset for the foot," but supposedly a woman who wears it can experience a kind of euphoria. She quotes Madonna as saying that Manolo Blahniks are as good as sex and "last longer."

Shoes can also become the symbol of one's core identity. You've met the person who is a runner and wears sneakers all the time, everywhere—from the garden to church. Running is her life and the sneakers are her anchor. They say, "This is not only what I do, it's what I am."

If you are uncomfortable in your clothes, you will be demonstrably less confident. Your body language will bleed that discomfort. All the world is a stage and clothing merely costume. But the costume sends messages about the character.

Move Toward the Holistic

"Review" is its own, complete exercise. Look at people around you and catalog similarities and differences. Gather your own pictures of people, and then review them as you become more and more conscious of your filters and how they affect your judgments of body language. You need to move to a point at which you can look clinically at people.

What you don't want to do is create Frankenstein's monster in using body language—piecing together hands, eyes, feet, and words to create an incongruous picture. What you do want is a catalog of the elements—like the colors in a portrait—that allow you begin to see how culture, habits, and involuntary movements come together to show you who the person really is and what she means to communicate.

4

Signaling, With or Without Intent

Continue to keep your mind on "review" in this chapter. You are in data-collection mode and the information we are giving you is to open your eyes—nothing more.

There are few absolutes in body language and we will flag those when we cover them. As for other movements, the first explanation of their meaning is "It depends..."

As a species we signal with the same set of tools, albeit in different ways. You will still be looking at isolated movements in this chapter, but from a different angle. In some cases, you'll go behind the signal to examine intent, and in others, you'll go behind the signal to see why it "just happens," that is, there is no intent.

This activity is still part of what interrogators call *passive observation*, which means watching the source to collect a range of useful information. It's like primatologist Jane Goodall observing the chimps by living among them. *Active observation* follows it and involves asking questions of people around the source, such as fellow prisoners and prison guards. It isn't until after those stages are complete that we move beyond observation and into evaluation, analysis, and decisions—the "E.A.D." in R.E.A.D. Everything related to "R" is an external process and everything related to "E.A.D." reflects internal processes.

In teaching body language, we categorize certain facial expressions that relate to seven specific emotions: disgust, sadness, anger, fear, surprise, contempt, and happiness. They are based on the work of psychologist Paul Ekman, who went around the world and tested the theory of universal expressions with people in different countries and different cultures. It was the foundation for a lifetime of discovery regarding the expression of human emotion.

The categories of signals are gestures, illustrators, regulators, adaptors, and barriers. We also associate mirroring with this group because it is a standard technique, which can be involuntary or intentional, for forging a bond with someone. Gestures and mirroring have their roots in culture, whereas the others are more universal expressions. We put rituals in this discussion as well, because they are movements people repeat that may have enormous meaning, or they may have no meaning whatsoever. (Also, they may be standard for an entire culture or they may be standard for a single individual).

Facial Expressions

Facial expressions have some absolutes. In fact, these are species absolutes for humans and they differ little by culture. By giving you photos of the seven emotions, we're giving you the same, simple test that has been administered in hundreds of different experimental efforts. Identify each of the emotions based on the previous list.

Both of us have taken large groups of people, put them in twos, and had one person face the slide with names of emotions on them, and one person with her back to the screen. We call out one of the emotions; the person with her back to the screen expresses that emotion with her face. The other person merely observes. After that, when we flash photos like this that capture each emotion, there are always gasps and "Yes!" from audience members. In every case, the person did something exactly like this, or something so similar that it was clearly recognizable.

But culture comes into play here, as with every other type of body language. When Ekman was interviewing Japanese people, he found that the intensity of their emotional expressions in session with him was quite low. In other words, their expressions were extremely muted. By putting the same subjects in a room by themselves and having them express various emotions, he discovered that it wasn't that they didn't express the basic emotions the same way as anyone else, it was that they didn't express them that way in the presence of someone whom they perceived to be an authority figure.

Greg saw this play out when living in the Republic of Korea as a young soldier before his interrogator days. His roommate, an ROK soldier, and fellow ROK soldiers were being addressed by the First Sergeant for missing formation. The body language was distinct: The soldier stood rigid with his hand down to his side even when struck. Greg thought this was an anomaly among the unit until nearly two decades later when he saw the same body language as a Korean American soldier was disciplined verbally by another Korean American U.S. Army Reserve officer. Though both were very well integrated into U.S. Army culture, the old ways of home were still prevalent.

Now consider the culture of your work environment, for example. If you work in a place where there is a concern about being fired for a politically incorrect remark, open display of disapproval, or any other level of indiscretion, it is possible that you will become practiced in muting responses. It doesn't mean you don't have intense emotion; you just know how not show it. You may or may not be Japanese, but your culture encourages you to suppress the expression of emotion. No matter how much it's muted, though, it's still visible.

Facial Expressions and Animals

Whether they are doing it intentionally or unintentionally, people around you are looking at your face for clues to your emotions and thoughts. But it is not those people who may be doing the best job of it—it is animals.

A study published in *Biology Letters* in February 2016 documented that horses reacted differently to photographs of positive versus negative human facial expressions.

> When viewing angry faces, horses looked more with their left eye, a behavior associated with perceiving negative stimuli. Their heart rate also increased more quickly and they showed more stress-related behaviors...this response indicates that the horses had a functionally relevant understanding of the angry faces they were seeing. The effect of facial expressions on heart rate has not been seen before in interactions between animals and humans.[1]

Why the left eye and not the right? Research with many species indicates that they view negative events with the left eye because information from the left eye is processed in the right hemisphere of the brain, the part that deals with threatening stimuli.

Horses are sensitive enough to a human being's emotional state and the expression of it that Equine-Facilitated Psychotherapy (EFP) is a growing adjunct to other types of mental health therapies. EFP is an experiential form of psychotherapy that relies on the horse's ability to see, smell, and feel changes in a person's emotional state throughout the time they are in contact with one another.[2]

The same month that the Sussex study on horses reading human emotions was published, the results of a study on dogs doing the same thing was announced. Dr. Kun Guo of the University of Lincoln's School of Psychology told Reuters that his research shows "dogs can integrate visual and oratory inputs to understand or differentiate human emotion as dog emotion."[3]

And then there's the marmoset, a New World monkey of which there are 22 varieties. Many are so tiny that they weigh less than half a pound, but their fully formed, five-fingered hands are one of many obvious signs that they are primates. Greg decided to do an unofficial body language test with a friend's marmoset to see if he could read human emotions.

The marmoset was on the floor, looking up—way up, since he's only about 6 inches tall—at Greg to make eye contact. Greg dropped his jaw and looked shocked as he looked past the little creature. The marmoset looked behind him. Greg repeated the test; again, the marmoset looked behind him as if he perceived that Greg had communicated "Watch out! There's a threat behind you!" Given that the marmoset is a primate, there may be other shared communication coding that Greg and the marmoset have in common. We'll have to report on that in another book. Just like this marmoset, you have the ability to read these seven expressions of emotion hardwired into your brain, so relax and let your instincts do some of the work.

Emotion From the Neck Down

If the face sends a message, the body compounds it. The body language from the neck down of each of the seven emotions is one way that, regardless of how reserved the facial expression is, the person experiencing the emotion is leaking that feeling through hands, feet, torso, and other body parts.

What emotions would you associate with the following body language?

Even though there are times when the "missing head" could convey another meaning, if the missing head in these examples were neutral, you would probably still get, respectively, sadness, fear, and contempt. Why?

The man in the top photo looks like a strong, young guy, but all of the power has drained out of his body. He is immersed in something that makes him feel weak and self-reflective. You can see from the angle of his upper body that he is slumped, which means his head is tilted forward.

The woman in the bottom left is clutching her bag and her jacket, as if to close her jacket even more tightly. These are protective gestures. You can also see that she is angled to the side as though she sees something that is causing her to be cautious, or even fearful. If you live in an urban environment, watch for this posture among subway riders. People who ride the train every day won't show it, but people who are new to the experience will probably show these signs of mild fear.

On the bottom right is a woman who has her arms folded with conviction. Someone or something has caused a sense of contempt to overtake her. Notice those weapons—her hands—are not trapped. That is a sure sign this is not simply a pose of comfort.

Exercise

Sit at a table in a crowded place like a coffee shop. Watch how people move their arms, shift the weight in their hips, jingle the keys in their pockets, pretend to do something with their cell phones, and tap their feet. Guess what their faces might look like.

Look up and see if there is a match between what the body is doing and what the face is expressing. In the cases where the body and face don't match, pay attention to whether or not the person is talking with someone (and being polite, for example) or acts as though she's being watched. In both cases, you will see a difference between face and body, but the body is giving you clues as to what the face would be doing if the person were honestly expressing emotion.

Now watch someone talking passionately on a mobile phone. Notice how much more animated the body language is although their focus is on the microphone. You might see hands flailing, brow moving, and maybe adapting and barriering. What is the message? Now look at the face. Which of the seven emotions is the person signaling? Why is that messaging so pronounced when no one is around? As we proceed to the categories of signals, think about how they might help convey the seven emotions discussed in the section on facial expressions.

Remember you are still in review. This is a laundry list of what to look for. In its very nature there are areas of discussion about what a signal can mean, but the purpose is to allow you to catalog and label the actions you see for later analysis.

Gestures

This is a category of absolutes. You either absolutely understand the gesture or you absolutely do not.

Gestures such as a kiss, sticking out your tongue, and waving hello capture particular sentiments. Gestures similar to these are learned expression of thought and can vary sharply from culture to culture. In every case, though, they represent a whole thought and convey a standard meaning as long as you replicate the context for them. For example, if you ask a question to which the answer is "yes," you will always understand that nodding means "yes," if the context is correct:

- You both understand the language being used.
- You're asking an American and nodding means "yes" for most people in the United States.
- The up and down movements in the nod are done in relatively quick succession.

Although a gesture is very cultural, as the culture spreads, it can become super-cultural. A good example is "thumbs up," which international peace-keeping troops with no single, common language can use with each other. It's not a good idea to use it if you happen to be in Iran, however. As a foreigner, you can only hope you would be forgiven for not knowing that it's like giving the middle finger there (and in many other parts of the world). That middle finger gesture would also be understood if you traveled back in time to the Roman Empire where flashing the *digitus impudicus*, or "impudent finger" signified contempt. Contrast that with the many interpretations of the fingers raised in a "V." To Americans who served in World War II, they see "victory." To baby boomers, it's a peace sign. To a lot of Brits, it is a way of flipping someone off if done with the back of the hand toward the person. The supposed root of this is that warriors would display their V-shaped fingers to the dying enemy they had just hit with an arrow. The two fingers they held up had released the deadly shaft.

Symbolic gestures can become a rich unspoken language when the gestures carry a clear and succinct meaning, as is the case in military hand signals, such as the "cover me" example in the previous chapter. The driving point is: Through some cultural change, all communicating parties learn the accepted meaning.

Gestures need all parties to understand and assign meaning to be useful. You cannot suddenly develop your own gesture and expect the world to understand it. High-performing groups develop insular gestures all the time. New body language signaling carries meaning in that group. As a person leaves that group and moves to a new group those gestures may leave the person lacking in ability to communicate as effectively, and if he uses the gesture he will appear to be out of touch. Unless he is alpha!

Illustrators and Regulators

Illustrators and regulators are punctuation. Their proper use and power may be learned by watching mom or dad, or people on TV—that is, culture influences the shape of them—but they are still a type of signal that comes "naturally." Watch a small child learning to communicate. The child will use her hands and feet to punctuate a thought as she storms off stamping her feet, flails her arms at the candy counter, or any other unscripted movements. Illustrators are the most natural human communication. Examples of illustrators are finger-pointing as you accuse a person of something and using your forearm to drive home your point. Regulators include using your hand similar to a stop sign or dragging your extended fingers across your throat to say, "Cut."

One of the classic signs of punctuating a message is batoning. Former President Bill Clinton used this illustrator in his public rebuttal of the accusation that he'd had an affair with Monica Lewinsky. His batoning forearm and extended index finger emphasized every word of his denial. After that, he started to place his thumb on his curled forefinger as he batoned instead of the accusatory pointed index finger, a move Greg calls "Clinton batoning," which has since been replicated by many politicians. Adolph Hitler did it as part of his wild gesticulation that whipped his audience into submission. Television evangelists do it to hammer on each and every word in a key Bible passage.

Watching the 2016 primaries, it was clear that the candidates had heard of batoning as an effective tool to drive home a point. In fact, body language commentary has created such a stir that most of the people in the early Republican debates could not figure out what to do with his or her hands while they attempt to baton. A typical progression was from no fingers extended, to one finger, then two, then three. Some candidates even stuck all their fingers out as though glued together and delivered military-style batoning. It was awkward to say the least. In contrast, Donald Trump used the okay sign as an illustrator, almost like flashing a gang sign.

Although signaling with gestures must be learned, illustrators do not have to be learned. Any movement can become an illustrator if used to drive home the message. Watch as a sassy teenager throws a shirt on the counter and huffs out of the store. Even if she never says "I don't have time to wait for a dressing room!" her action illustrates her thoughts. Even a gesture such as flashing the middle finger can become an illustrator when used to punctuate thoughts. Other examples of illustrators are:

- Finger pointing, either as an accusation or a designation.
- Use of any body part to baton, such as a head tilt, finger wag, foot shake, or movement of the entire upper body.
- Opening the lips to overly enunciate each word.
- Closing the lips and tilting the head as you slowly speak to someone who doesn't get it.
- Placing the palms together in a prayerful motion as you plead your case.
- Placing the fingers to the lips while thinking.

Bill O'Reilly uses regulators all the time, as do most of the news talk hosts who invite argument. When he's had his fill of a guest's comments, the hand goes up and he may slightly tilt his head, barrier with the eyelids, and jump in with his viewpoint. If he can't shut him up that way, he may combine both hands with a facial gesture that says "Enough": raised eyebrows, pursed lips, set jaw.

Regulators do not need to be elaborate or well understood. Any signal that has an effect on the cadence of another person, managing whose turn it is to speak, volume, or continuing of a conversation can be a regulator. Some are formal, while others are impromptu. Simply questioning someone's veracity has the effect of slowing or halting a line of conversation. For example:

- "Talk to the hand."
- A shocked gasp.
- A roll of the eyes.
- Placing the hands to the pain muscle.
- Looking up while exhaling.

Other simple and common versions of the regulator include:

- Pointing to someone as if to say "Your turn."
- Placing your hand on someone.

- Tilting the head to indicate interest (a very female regulator).
- Simply nodding as someone speaks to encourage that behavior.
- Shaking the head to discourage behavior.

Adaptors

Adaptors are a way that the body tries to comfort itself. It is a way to create familiar in the unfamiliar. The primary cause of this is discomfort due to a real or perceived threat or boredom. The body will invent innumerable ways to do this, but in true human fashion, we have developed standard ways as well. Because adaptors are often so gender-specific, we will go into greater detail about them in the discussion of filters. The key thing to know at this stage is that reflecting energy displacement is a way to relieve stress. Because it comforts, the use of an adaptor—more than any other piece of body language—can become a habit and result in strange or idiosyncratic behavior.

Why does a baseball player rub his legs before grabbing the bat?

a. Wipe the sweat off his hands.

b. Wipe the dirt off his hands.

c. Relieve stress.

He has gloves and pine tar on his hands, so he isn't doing (a) or (b). The gesture is (c), an adaptor.

Other examples of adaptors are:

- Fidgeting of nearly any kind.
- Rubbing fingertips together.
- Wobbling legs back and forth while seated (a very male adaptor).
- Tapping.
- Scratching.
- Grooming.
- Picking.
- Rubbing a body part.

Barriers

Barriers create space, whether real or ritual. Barriers often show you are uncomfortable with a threat. People find scores of ways to block out the offender. Here are some examples, although we should point out that doing one of these things doesn't necessarily make it a barrier. Context is all-important.

- Standing behind a table.
- Crossing your arms.
- Turning sideways while in conversation.
- Putting your purse or briefcase between you and the other person.
- Lowering your eyelids during a conversation.
- Putting your arm on a table between you and the person next to you.
- Holding up reading materials.

Barriers can also make you seem "untouchable" by helping to expand your personal space. Sitting behind a desk to interview someone for a job is using a barrier to convey power. You control more area than she does.

As noted in Chapter 3, a common protective movement men use is to barrier the genitals by crossing their hands. Watch men on TV game shows who are unaccustomed to making public appearances. Even though some of them are behind a podium, you will see their hands down in a fig-leaf position— that's a double barrier. It's a natural movement for men to cover their genitals when they are under any kind of stress.

One of the news stories of 2005 involved a monkey who attacked a California man who had brought a birthday cake to the animal sanctuary for another monkey. Feeling threatened—the birthday monkey had earned 39 candles, so it must have been a blazing cake—the attacking monkey did what came naturally: He ripped the testicles off his adversary. Alpha-males do things similar to this, which is why "protecting the precious" is a posture ingrained in men. No thought is involved; it's pure instinct.

Driving through the outskirts of a small town, Greg encountered a line of three cars that had been stopped by a woman on the road crew. She and her counterpart about two-tenths of a mile down the road relayed the status to each other; one would flash her "slow" sign while the other flashed her "stop" sign so that one lane of traffic could move through at all times. For some reason, Greg's side of the line continued to stare at a "stop" sign for more than a minute, which was apparently too much for the drivers at the front of the line. They did U-turns.

It was too much for the stop-sign holder as well. She held up the sign in front of her face, and then put it down to talk on the radio as she turned her back. She was embarrassed, helpless, guilty; she took this personally. Another few words on the radio. Her body language communicated, "Please give me back some control. Let the people on my side go!" She didn't make eye contact until she flipped the sign to "slow" and waved the line forward.

Her gestures showed that her mind was looking for an outlet, an immediate answer to "What do I do to get out of this uncomfortable situation?" Her solution was to use everything around her as a barrier between her and the people she presumed were judging her: the stop/slow sign, her radio, her helmet that partly shielded her eyes, and her back.

You will commonly see behavior similar to this with a nervous speaker, who also presumes that everyone in this audience is judging him. In his mind, the barriers protect him from scrutiny: He stands behind the podium with the microphone angled to cover a portion of his face, and his hands lift the papers he's reading to further obscure him. If he's wearing glasses, the audience might see nothing but ears and hair the whole time he's presenting.

In contrast to the nervous speaker's unconscious reliance on barriers, consider the use of barriers in conflict. In that context, they are used consciously and deliberately after a threat has been identified. Bill C. Berger is an historical novelist with a background in martial arts and other close combat. In his forthcoming novel, *Doll*, he describes the tactical use of barriers in fighting:

> Martial artists train to work angles. The most basic defensive technique in virtually all fighting styles involves putting something between the fighter and his opponent along the most common angle of attack. Boxers put hands before their chests and faces. Swordsmen put blades before them for the same reason. By having hands or weapons already placed along the angle of attack, a martial artist is able to block quickly.[4]

Barriers, therefore, can be part of a defensive or offensive approach to a person or set of circumstances. The problem with barriers as offense is they can block your vision to the real message from the opponent. You can't see through a metal shield.

This introduction to *The Big 5*—gestures, illustrators, regulators, adaptors, and barriers—isn't intended to be comprehensive. Its primary value is to give you a tool to observe and catalog what you are seeing for later use as you try to decide what this means. These categories allow you to think about the actions people take. Some are intentional, like gestures. Others are so innate, we do not even realize we are doing them; that would include adaptors, illustrators, and barriers. Finally, regulators are either intentional or accidental. If you learn nothing more about body language, you will have started an effective internal dialogue to string together body language phrases into a sentence instead of reading a single element, like crossed arms, as an entire sentence. The better you understand these parts of the body language sentence, the less likely you are to instinctively do something and the more likely you are to send the message you intended.

If *The Big 5* are the fundamental units of body language, the next two are the DNA of human behavior. Because they are so fundamental to who we are, we rarely even notice the impact. By simply learning how to recognize and catalog these two categories Greg calls *meta-behaviors*, you we will read deeper into your subject. By learning to harness these in yourself or others, you are tapping into something much deeper than mere body language.

Mirroring

At its base, mirroring is simply emulating behavior. Mirroring can be a learned behavior, but typically, it is nothing more than assimilation. Mirroring is a natural response to your culture; that's how we get to be homogeneous as a society. This is *adaptational mirroring*. Mirroring the super-typical is a natural response to social norming. The yawn is an evolutionary mirroring response and a powerful tool to break the ice and build rapport.

We commonly get rewards—pay raises, compliments, and invitations to events—from other people in our culture when we behave like them. And when we don't become them, we are punished. High-pressure social norming is the *requirement* to mirror the behavior of others or face extremely unpleasant consequences. That's what happens with Stockholm syndrome. U.S. military basic training relies on a modified version of Stockholm syndrome. The components are these: One man uses ritualistic rage to intimidate you, to control every moment of your life, and forces you to become like him. The new guy is like an ape thrown into a cage with 27 others who all know who the alpha is and what pleases him. You are the 28th ape who must try to figure that out so that the alpha doesn't tear your testicles off. So, you start to mimic him.

There are parallels in religious indoctrination, although what many people experience is a level of intimation through ritual, but not ritualistic rage. Some children have the "fear of God" put in them and try to avert the "wrath of God" by mimicking the actions of religious leaders, parents, and other people who have a lot of practice doing it.

There is also intentional mirroring. That is part of manipulation to subliminally suggest a connection with another person. In Part III, we will tell you how to use it so that it looks natural.

Rituals

Rituals range from formalized bits of ceremony to micro-cultural norms to personal habits. Sometimes, we know their origins and purpose, and sometimes we don't have a clue, but we do them anyway. Both of us have a strong background in theater and are well-schooled in the shared superstitions of performing artists. The one that's probably the most well-known, even among non-thespians, is wishing a performer good luck by saying, "Break a leg." Saying "Good luck!" is bad luck. One probable source of the ritualistic phrase is that successful performance elicits sustained applause and as long as the clapping continues, the actors move onstage, offstage, and onstage again. Each time, they "break the legs," which is the name for the narrow drapes used to mask the wings of the stage.

If you are a non-Catholic and you have ever attended a Catholic Mass, you know you're an outsider because you don't know the rituals of the hundreds of other people in that church. And if you decide to watch a baseball game and know nothing about the rituals of baseball, you might wonder if there is jealously or just childish behavior going on when a pitcher with a no-hitter seems to be snubbed by all of his teammates in the dugout. The ritual is: Don't talk to, sit near, stare at, or breathe near that pitcher or you could break his streak.

There are also numerous cultural norms related to proximity to another person, signs of respect for people in authority, and so on. One arcane norm that relates to space, as well as eye contact, plays out in public bathrooms every day. In the average urinal in America—and this is not something that women personally witness—men follow the "urinal rules." Rule #1: Do not look down over the barrier. Rule #2: Conversation with strangers concurrently using the urinal is not acceptable. Rule #3: If you want to talk with the man you've spotted while you're both at the urinal—maybe you want to know where he got his tie—wait until you both get to the sink and you're washing your hands. Is this the same for all men? Of course not, but it is a valid generalization because it fits a huge chunk of the population.

Two people in a relationship will commonly develop microcultural rituals to show affection, anger, boredom, and so on. When you extricate yourself from a long-term relationship, part of the baggage you take along is the signs and rituals that you developed in the context of that relationship. These may come back to haunt the next relationship.

Personal rituals that affect *primary human drivers* (food, sex, and sleep) are profound. They also serve to illustrate how people create personal rituals around everyday activities. As you are learning to catalog behaviors, do this: For the next several days make notes, mental or written, about how you approach the table, create "sacred space" around food and eating, and close out your meal. Let's say you are a fast eater; chewing happens occasionally. Or you always sit from the right side of the chair and rotate in counterclockwise versus pulling the chair out. Make note of these routines and habits for a few days. The way you approach meals serves your need for both comfort and ritual. Now do the same for preparing for bed and for sex. Did you notice patterns? These are personal rituals. These are among the most profound, but we ritualize many things. Disturbing those rituals creates chaos and brings out barriers and adaptors. Now start cataloging rituals that you see from the person. Just remember that sometimes what you see isn't a ritual at all, but rather something the person has done once or twice.

Some signals have taken on meaning through cultural context and you can only truly understand them as part of that culture. Then again, as advertising and media span the globe, some cultural gestures or icons have become ubiquitous and super-cultural, such as the name Coca-Cola, the word *okay*, and the middle-finger gesture.

Other very specific signaling can result from a group's evolution, and this can be observed at horse auctions, for example. Most new people are almost wooden the first few times they go an auction such as this. They are afraid of signaling. Good auctioneers know the itchy nose scratch from the bid nose scratch, though. They see the intensity of the gaze and contact made between the auctioneer and bidder.

In becoming a skilled practitioner of reading body language, you need to become the auctioneer. This means looking for the other pieces of body language when you see what looks like a gesture. Is there focus of energy? Does the person have eye contact? What does the rest of the body say? No single gesture or flinch can tell you something when it stands alone, unless it is a piece of symbolic language, such as the middle finger. Even when you see such a symbol, you must be like the auctioneer and say to yourself "Does this person look like a seasoned auction attendee, or just someone here for a weekend of entertainment?"

Take a few minutes and start to think about how you catalog the individual movements of the person or people you are reviewing. We have looked at the big picture and how the actors are interacting with one another. Now start to list the individual movements and put them into labeled boxes. Is the action one of *The Big 5*, or does it fit into a different category? Is this person deliberately mirroring to be one of the cool kids? Is this something so ingrained that it has become ritualistic?

By cataloging what you have seen from the top to the bottom you are starting to form a holistic picture instead of focusing on the individual parts. You are getting the verbs, nouns, adjectives, and adverbs of the body language sentence. Now let's start to discuss prepositions and articles in body language to tie the elements of your developing catalog together.

The Holistic View

Reading and understanding body language starts with an inside-out look at *yourself*. The ability to use your body language to manipulate others starts with an inside-out look at *other people*. So we're at a bridge in this chapter: an inside-out look that enhances your ability to read, understand, and use body language.

For that reason, midway through the chapter, we switch from "R" to "E"— evaluate. It's the point at which we focus your attention on mood, energy, and posture. These are the elements of body language that tincture and tie everything else together. Combined with your knowledge of movements, it will help you develop a holistic view of another person's body language.

With this chapter, we help you leave the pure cataloging of what you see and start using your brain to evaluate some of that data. But in order to take that step, it's important to know a little more about how the human brain works.

Artifact Versus Icon Thinker

Claudia Mazzucco, a high-functioning autistic and well-known expert on the history of golf, has received glowing reviews for her debut book, *Legendary Lessons* (Skyhorse, 2016), which features golf teachings from many of "the greats" of yesteryear. But it's her personal story of discovering her talents in spite of—or perhaps because of—autism that brings us into close contact with the mind of someone who has accessed an understanding of human movement and intention in a very different way from most of us. Her article entitled "Lost in Autism, Found by Golf" for *Golf Digest*'s "Golf Saved My Life" series, is introduced by the sentence: "Mazzucco is drawn to golf for its statistics and peace of mind."[1]

Claudia, who was born in Argentina, is not a player; playing golf involves conversation and interaction. She is a golf historian whose intimate knowledge of human movement and intention doesn't come from real-time interaction with people, but rather by reading and reflection, by being "alone with the authors and characters in the wonderful world of golf."[2]

> When I was 17, I moved to Buenos Aires to live with family and studied to become a journalist. The city overwhelmed me. I went for walks in the park because it was quiet. One day I came across the Campo de Golf de la Ciudad, a public course in the middle of Palermo Park. It was so peaceful! I used to go just to walk and sit.

> For class, we had to research something that interested us. I told PGA of Argentina that I wanted to do a project on golf history and asked if I could look around. Their records were very poor, so I went to the library in Buenos Aires looked through newspapers. I recorded the scores of every player, in every round, in every major tournament in Argentina. I went all the way back to 1905.

> I loved it. I was captivated by numbers and had a photographic memory for dates and names so this was a perfect fit for me. Knowing no one else who could do such mundane work, the golf association happily paid me. The project took 13 years to finish. I then became the librarian at the Argentina Golf Association.[3]

Claudia is what Greg calls an *artifact thinker*, that is, someone who sees discrete packages of information; everything is individually representative. So with all her in-depth knowledge of what makes a golfer a great golfer, why doesn't Claudia Mazzucco play? As an artifact thinker, she is a repository of "how things got to this point" and "who played what part." She can separate facts from reasons, but application of the facts presents a formidable challenge.

Exploring briefly how Claudia sees people and what they do gives us a point on the far end of the continuum of innate abilities to read body language. We all fall somewhere on that continuum, and as you get familiar with the R.E.A.D. system, if you have certain challenges or don't get the results you think you should get, consider that everyone has a different "normal." Claudia approaches her understanding of human behavior very differently from how many of us do—and it isn't through observation of real people! Her preferred way to understand the R.E.A.D. system, for example, is by reading.

I do not think that I've learned over the course of time to read people's body language by observation. I've never had any clue what people might be suggesting through their movements. There was little reason to do so. During childhood and adolescence, in the small town of La Banda, it was rare to encounter people whose body language was essential to understand a given situation. I've spent my entire life learning about people in the context of books and stories or movies and TV. I learn about people's inside stories. I quickly discovered that story will provide me with every detail that I needed to understand what a situation is about. I've always gotten very anxious when people show emotions through their body language. I tried to avoid them. I get scared and run away.

It did not surprise me that body language can be learned. I would rather like to know how a study of body language can be instrumented. The fact that your [Maryann's] friend's daughter is very good at reading body language now comes only to reinforce my idea or conclusion that people with autism can indeed learn about anything in regard to human relationships, create and maintain positive relationships and function pretty well in community.[4]

Now for a sharp contrast: An autistic person like Claudia has a high gray-to-white matter ratio in her brain (more on this in a moment). Conspiracyclub is a group of people with too much white matter. They give us "9 Clues indicating Orlando Mass Shooting Is a False Flag Operation" (that is, the FBI staged a shooting at a gay nightclub to scare us and 50 people weren't really killed) and "The Oldest Man in the World 256 Years Breaks The Silence Before His Death" (that is, with the right herbs and good breathing techniques, you too can live as long as a deep-sea clam).[5]

Just as Greg has a name for the way Claudia Mazzucco thinks, he also has a name for the way these conspiracy theorists process information: They are *icon thinkers* in the extreme. Exact opposites of the artifact thinkers, these are people who see correlations between pieces of information whether or not they are verifiable. A certain amount of this ability is essential and useful, of course, because it's the white matter that helps us create meaning, stories, and relationships out of what we perceive. In terms of reading body language, unlike Claudia who can't seem to put the pieces and parts together, these folks are more likely to turn every nose scratch into a sign of lying or more.

If you doubt that a lot of people buy into conspiracy theories, consider the study "Conspiracy Theories and the Paranoid Style(s) of Mass Opinion," published in the March 2014 *American Journal of Political Science*. In the study some researchers from the University of Chicago took an unprecedented look at the nature of mass public support for conspiracy theories. Their conclusion: "Using four nationally representative surveys, sampled between 2006 and 2011, we find that half of the American public consistently endorses at least one conspiracy theory."[6]

That's a lot of people with excess white matter. What's going on in their heads? More importantly, where do *you* fit on the continuum of artifact thinker to icon thinker?

Icons carry more meaning that what is literally there. A crucifix is not just a piece of wood with the sculpture of a male body nailed to it. To Christians, it is the story of the Son of God dying to redeem mankind. For many, it stirs emotions and stories of suffering, salvation, and miracles. In other words, this icon of Christianity is a piece of art that is more than the sum of its parts. To the extreme artifact thinker, the crucifix *is* the sum of its parts. It might be oak and bronze carved and assembled to present the image of a man on a cross. The extreme artifact thinker has healthy qualities; each episode in life isn't necessarily tied to the next. The problem becomes when an artifact thinker applies lessons learned from reading a book about one person's interaction and it becomes everyone's interaction. It creates an absolutist mindset to the world around them.

Remember we are talking about behavior and not brain-imaging results. Too far in either direction of icon or artifact isn't healthy. Most of us are somewhere in the middle, capable of making snap judgments that "x = y" is an absolute, and then a few hours later, changing our mind. One minute Elvis Presley was the embodiment of Rock and Roll, and then based on new evidence, we suddenly believe he is still alive and leading a cult of ancient aliens in Area 51.

Before going any further, let's look at a few brain basics. Generally, scientists describe your brain as having three parts: a cerebrum, a cerebellum, and a brainstem. The cerebrum has two hemispheres, right and left. That's where you find white and gray matter. The tucks and folds of gray matter have huge involvement in memory, attention, perceptual awareness, thought, language, and consciousness.[7] Most of the oxygen we breathe that makes it to brain heads straight for the gray matter. But with "normal" individuals, gray matter occupies just 40 percent of the cerebrum, with white matter filling up the other 60 percent. To make the relationships a little simpler to grasp, Greg often describes gray matter as the computer and white matter as the network. According to *Medical Daily*,

> Gray matter areas of the nervous system sit on top of white matter, which is composed mostly of long nerve fibers enveloped by a myelin sheath. The myelin gives it the white color and helps move signals along nerve axons. Gray matter contains the bodies of the nerve cells. The cerebral cortex is entirely composed of gray matter. White matter contains core structures, such as the thalamus and hypothalamus; one of its jobs is relaying sensory information from the rest of the body to the cerebral cortex. White matter also has an integral role in regulating autonomic (automatic, or unconscious) body functions like heart rate. With this description in mind, you might think of the brain working from the inside out, therefore: "The inner white matter allows communication to and from gray matter areas, and between the gray matter and the other parts of the body, while the processing of information is concluded in the outer layer of gray matter. Perhaps for these reasons, sex differences in white and gray matter sometimes inspire controversy."[8]

Remember that we're talking about "normal" brains, because what the brain indicates in imaging studies is that "normal" women have more gray matter than "normal" men. There are plenty of nuances involved with this fact, however, and among them are head size and the number of connections running between the right and left hemispheres.

The important point for you to note is that both gray and white matter perform vital functions in terms of the four elements of R.E.A.D. If your brain—because of genetics, chronic stress, disease, or other factors—doesn't have what we might call a balance between gray and white matter, then your view of body language will probably reflect that.

Now flip that around. What if you are trying to read someone who collects and interacts with information very differently from you? Your filters will affect how you perceive that individual.

Depression and Masking

Among their peers, people suffering from serious depression often say a depressed person is a natural actor. They are often asked "Are you okay?" and they learn to put on the soldier's face and say "Yes," even though they are suffering inside. Often the reason they are perceived as great actors is the person doing the asking desperately wants the answer the person is giving. The neuro-typical non-depressed person is looking for some way to understand the depressed person and gives him an out. In this way, the "acting" body language is accepted as normal, when, in fact, the face of depression isn't normal.

Psychologist Paul Ekman's work in micro-expressions—split-second expressions of emotion that are uncontrollable and involuntary—originated from his work with severely depressed individuals who were "acting." Some young psychiatrists had asked Ekman whether he could help identify when a suicidal patient was telling the truth or lying about improving. They were reluctant to give out weekend passes because they'd seen too many unfortunate outcomes. Ekman knew from these psychiatrists that some patients had left the hospital and killed themselves within an hour of arriving back home.

Ekman began his work with a patient named Mary. She had attempted suicide three times before she met him. When he taped his first session with her, she smiled and seemed to be very cheery. The reality, which he didn't know at the time, was that she was angling for a weekend pass so that she could go home and kill herself. After building trust with Mary, she ultimately confessed to Ekman that she'd been lying during a previous interview he had filmed. She admitted that her true intention was to get out of the hospital and kill herself.

Ekman looked the film, but he didn't see any evidence of her lying. So he went through it frame by frame for a week, and micro-expressions of despair showed up in two instances. Each was a 25th of a second, out of a 12-minute film. This tedious exercise is how Ekman learned that the human subjects he studied betrayed their true emotional state, no matter how much they tried to suppress it.

The Pattern Trap

The normal human tendency—that is, simplifying a concept more than a neuroscientist would, the tendency among people who have a normal ratio of gray-to-white matter—is to make judgments based on grouping things together. We are fundamentally pattern-finding animals. The people who survived to pass on their genes were successful at identifying threat and mitigating the risk, in part because of an ability to see patterns. Your impressions of people are most likely based on the aggregate presentation of a person. You get an overall impression that ranges from highly negative to highly positive.

That's a problem if you're trying to do analysis because you sometimes accept something that seems to belong to the picture when it actually doesn't belong. This is the reason for cataloging everything in the "review" stage. Conversely, you think you see something that ought to be there and it really isn't there. This is what happens when you're reading a sentence with a word missing but you don't notice it's missing because your brain assumes it's there.

Not only do we group things together, we do it in such a way that we put the pieces together in a pattern. The brain attempts to fill whatever blanks are there—or to "correct" elements—so that the pattern is complete and makes sense.

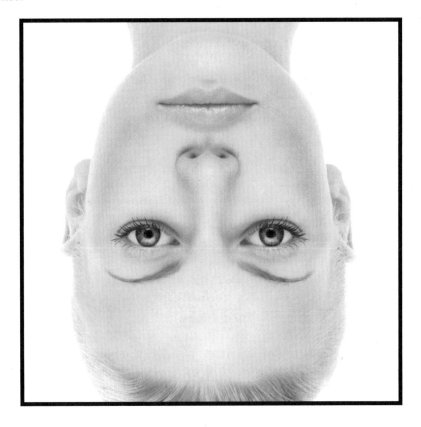

Aside from this image being upside down, what's wrong with it?

This is an example of the Thatcher effect. We're used to seeing faces in the upright position. When we see it upside down, we impose sense on it that isn't there, that is, we impose a pattern.

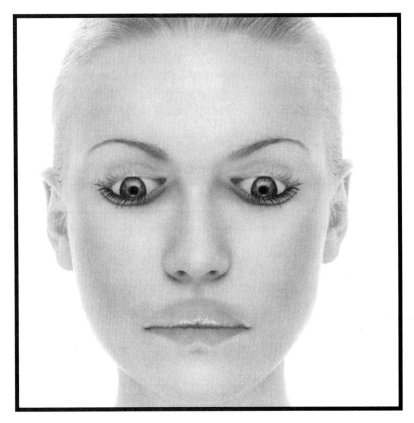

Here's the face upright.

The eyes and the mouth in the image are upside down, but most people don't pick that up when the entire head is inverted. Much of the time this kind of patterning activity occurs without your brain even knowing what's going on. On one hand, it reflects the brain's efficiency. On the other hand, it's a trap.

In some circumstances, if you didn't have this ability, your safety would be at risk. For example, in a survival situation, your ability to put the elements of a threat together to determine a course of action sometimes requires agility in pattern recognition. For example, if you're in an alpine environment and see broken twigs, large prints in mud, and bear scat, these are pieces of a pattern. You don't want to complete the pattern physically by having a bear show up. We are programed by nature to find threat where there is none. Humans who think that a rock is a bear might be paranoid, but those who think a bear is a rock will never live to reproduce.

Patternality [is] the ability to discern (and ultimately make) new patterns in the environment. Patternality is common to all life forms.

It represents a deep instinct, a drive, a need to impose order on the world so as to make it usable and survivable…. Patternality with its affordances shapes how we and all creatures make sense and meaning of the environment within which we exist and the world within which we live. At the biological level, it drives survivability. At the cognitive and social levels, it drives learning and meaning-making for humans and many other social species.[9]

But this powerful and extraordinary tendency to create patterns and "fill in the blanks" has a down side, too. Think back on the last horrible misunderstanding you experienced in a relationship with someone you care about or whose opinion you value. It's highly likely that your brain's predisposition toward filling in the blanks amplified, or even caused, the misunderstanding.

What the R.E.A.D. system does in the "R" section is help you notice component parts. Moving into the "E," you are starting to make sense of how movements work together, contradict each other, or run counter to what's coming out of the mouth. You are looking for what is normal for the culture, group, gender, or individual. Our tendency to create patterns out of what we see makes it difficult to do that. So keep the pattern trap in mind as you consider how people convey how they really feel (or don't) and what's really going on inside their head.

Remember: In this section we are talking about how your brain works and a few behavioral symptoms common to humans. This is intended to start an internal conversation about what you typically do and what you noticed that you might have missed by overlaying your brain on to the person or people you were reviewing. This is the first set of filters to strip.

You are not just like Jane Goodall, a human expert observing chimps. You are a chimp, too. It is the human condition that you are at a disadvantage in trying to be completely objective.

Since it is the human condition, let's discuss some emotional states that can affect the thinking and body language messaging of humans. You are now crossing the bridge to "E."

Mood

Since we are firmly in the "evaluate" stage, you need some tools to help look more closely at the catalog of behavior symptoms and environment you have created. From childhood our moods impact us like storms in the psychological landscape. They force us to make better or worse decisions, fall for or notice tricks and ploys, and they even affect our intellectual capacity. So mood must become a sculpting factor for any discussion of what a symptom might say. The R.E.A.D. system offers a framework to determine what the body is saying overall. It structures your observations.

Only a delusional person wakes up in the morning and declares, "Today, I will demonstrate clearly what I am thinking through body language!" Most of what happens is hardwired. We are good at blocking portions of our body language but not good at seeing ourselves as we are. This is based partly on the fact that we respond to positive and negative feedback to create a repertoire that works for us socially, both consciously and subconsciously. Remember the key message of the culture chapter: Unless we are alpha, we are emulating the alpha and overlaying it to our own catalog of gestures to maintain identity while keeping alpha happy. Even if we are alpha, we must constantly be wary of challengers and adapt, lest another become alpha and we drop to typical.

After years of study, training, and practice, Greg is an example of someone who can look across a crowded room and decipher a person's real state—the authentic mood inside. The R.E.A.D. system codifies what his brain does in those circumstances, and the intent is that it will help your brain learn to do the same with the added benefit of specialized knowledge you possess that he doesn't.

To begin, there are three parts to looking at the holistic body language of a person: energy, direction, and focus. We will use these to catalog moods.

1. **Energy:** How lively is the person? Does she look tired or invigorated? Is it normal or abnormal? When I say "energy," I am talking from head to toe, and even more than that. Bill Clinton has energy that showed even after his heart surgery. In his July 26, 2016 speech at the Democratic National Convention, he showed abundant energy that grew throughout the speech. His attempt to use the power of his rhetoric to humanize his wife, the party's choice for president, was effective on many levels. And it sent an important message about him as well as her: At two weeks from 70 years old and slathered in enough makeup to make a Kardashian cringe, he showed he could be as lively as President Bill Clinton of the 1990s. If we see that energy fail, it indicates that something is going on in his head to cause a downward shift.

2. **Direction:** Is the energy this person displays free-wheeling and all over the board? Is it sharply aimed at a common goal? Temper this perception with what is normal for the person. You cannot, for instance, look once at someone who is scatterbrained and assume there is a root cause other than genes.

3. **Focus:** Is the energy focused internally or externally? Is the person directed at getting away from something, or simply disconnected from those around him? This can tell us more about the mental state of someone than the other two combined.

These primary criteria form the foundation of this new system for looking holistically at a person. They serve as big-chunk categories in analyzing behavior. Let's wrap them in a simple label: mood indicators. Combined with the scalp-to-sole list and the checklist on posture that follows, you can get close to clarifying the meaning of a person's body language.

The concept is simple: Use the three elements to describe the overall effect that the scalp-to-sole elements present when they come together. For example:

- Energy is low or high.

- Direction answers the question: Are all of the arrows lined up? Is the person paying sharp attention to a person, place, or thing with all outward expression and the senses? Is all of that energy sharply directed at one target or scattered among several pre-occupying factors?

- Focus is either internal or external. It could be sharp or scattered relative to something apparent to the outside world, or the focus—sharp or scattered—could be on something inside his head.

The following table provides a sampling of moods or emotions, and a profile of them according to energy, direction, and focus.

Mood	Energy	Direction	Focus
Confusion	Low	Scattered	Internal
Distraction	High	Scattered	Internal
Anger	High	Sharp	External
Joy	High	Sharp	External
Excitement	High	Scattered	Stimulus dependent
Interest	High	Sharp	External
Fear	High	Sharp	External
Secretiveness	Low	Sharp	External
Embarrassment	Low	Sharp	Internal

Confusion

Energy low, direction scattered, focus internal.

A great movie moment that shows confusion is a key scene in *Braveheart*, the classic 1995 historical drama that won five Academy Awards. When Mel Gibson's character, William Wallace, discovers that Robert the Bruce has betrayed him, Wallace's preoccupation moves deep into the psyche—a depiction of internal focus. He seems so occupied that he may not even notice anything else. His mind has discovered something that threatens his very being, and that enemy has sapped his energy. There is suddenly an incongruity in his picture of the universe.

Distraction

Energy high, direction scattered, focus internal.

You wake up in the morning and know you will be late for work; you have too many things to do before you leave. You run around the house looking for keys, trying to remember what else you need to take with you. Nothing goes right.

People in this state may say they are confused, but the truth is, the mind has an overwhelming preoccupation: I'm late. This fixation prevents focus on anything else as long as the mind knows there is urgency at hand. Under these conditions, body language has no consistent direction, meaning the syntax of the body language is discordant, and not sending a unified signal.

Anger

Energy high, direction sharp, focus external.

Most people can recognize anger easily when it's openly expressed, but what if the person masks it? Are there still tell-tale signs? By using a whole-body approach and narrowing to the differences between anger and distraction or anger and fear, for example, you can find the signs. Begin by understanding what picture the canvas presents, and then looking at the individual colors— the hands, feet, eyes, lips, nose, and so on.

Anger involves an energy level so high that it seeps out, even when a person tries to mask it. The angry person has a consuming drive to deal with the cause. Direction is not an issue, either. This individual has unity of purpose in body and mind: Eliminate the cause of his anger.

In men, the direction manifests itself in physical displays of aggression, whether overt or masked. In women, this demonstration can simply be a sharpening of the wit or more feminine behavior, like CNN's conservative pundit S.E. Cupp fluttering her eyelashes at another female in the discussion. The commonality is hyper-demonstrative gender behavior. Women rarely fistfight; they "catfight" instead. Similar to cats, they pose and growl a lot, often with little contact other than the swipe of a claw. The subtlety can be missed on men. The result of this miss is played out in comedies in which these hyper-feminine behaviors become even more exaggerated.

Angry men have a decidedly external focus, in some cases even to the detriment of the well-cultivated persona. The old Southern gentleman can, indeed, be pushed to beat your ass in the parking lot. In women, this focus is never quite so narrow until rage, the next level of intensity, enters the picture. If men are prepared for hand-to-hand combat early on, women are prepared to fence. Women will typically focus on the cause while keeping in mind the preservation of species. By her very nature, a woman remains more cognitive than a man during times of anger, if not as in control. The root of this difference is the size of the amygdala, the brain structure associated with aggression. It's larger in men than in women, so although angry men move, angry women tend to observe and process. Similar to the cat, only in dire straits will the growling and hissing result in action.

Joy

Energy high, direction sharp, focus external.

So far, joy looks identical to anger. Because of their identical profiles, they are both easy to identify. The physiological difference is what part of brain is engaged, and the emotional difference can be described in terms of magnetism: Anger repels and joy attracts.

We describe joy as overwhelming happiness. Most of us would probably agree that "joy" is not something we typically associate with day-to-day soldier behavior. Greg and his Army buddies once played a horrible practical joke on a fellow soldier because they wanted to provoke this "unsoldierly" emotion. They copied this guy's numbers from a lottery ticket he left on a desk. Shortly after that, he came to ask if anyone knew the winning numbers. They sent him to the person he thought was the most credible guy in the unit, and this trusted source read off the numbers one by one. As the numbers matched he became progressively more excited. When he heard the last number, this balding, thick-waisted old soldier sprang into the air and kicked his feet like a boy. This reckless abandon of his personal image came crashing down when he looked into the next room and saw the other soldiers in their own perverted demonstrations of joy.

Depending on culture, people display high energy differently. For instance, an acceptable level of energy associated with joy in a young woman will elicit stares when used by a middle-aged man. When we sign a contract for a new publishing project, Maryann raises her hands past the shoulder and has a gleeful look on her face, with lots of energy bubbling to the highest parts of her body. Greg, on the other hand, smiles. It is a very large smile and his body becomes more animated. But there is a big difference between "joyful" and "gleeful" expressions. Living with military discipline since the age of 14, and raised by Southern parents, Greg displays the impact of layers of culture subculture and gender on a simple expression of joy. The perception from an early age is that men do not "flit about."

Similar to a person demonstrating anger, a person demonstrating joy stays focused on the cause. Direction of energy is unilateral. The only additional factor is whether the joy relates to something present or a past occurrence that has just come to the person's attention. Watch a person who has just learned of great news from a letter. Does she hold the letter as a relic in this ritual of celebration, or discard it and dance around? She holds on to it, most likely. When a person learns joy-causing news over the phone, all energy goes into the conversation. Even the eyes may find their way toward the phone. Every ounce of the person's being is concentrated on what she perceives as the source.

Again, similar to anger, the initial external focus can shift to the inside. In joy, it happens as the person relishes the impact of the profound event on his life: The new book contract causes a celebration, but the long-term effect of having a greater sense of purpose moves the joy inward. The focus may go strictly internal as the person tries to sustain the feeling of euphoria by thinking of all the spillover effects of the good news.

Excitement

Energy high, direction scattered, focus stimulus dependent.

Arguably, excitement is a category under which many of the other moods can fall. For a moment, suspend disbelief and imagine that excitement is only a single mood not caused by anger, joy, and so on. It's just a feeling that comes from your synapses firing.

As the happy-excited person comes to life, his center of gravity seems to rise, as though the weight of years is leaving. His face lights up and he seems desperate to communicate. This kind of excitement creates a youthful appearance even in the elderly, as the posture becomes more erect and pace of movement increases. Think of a child at Christmas, or even an adult at Christmas who anticipates receiving or giving the perfect gift. Or even former President Bill Clinton in his 2016 speech about his wife.

Excitement could also stem from anxiety, aggravation, or a number of other negatives. The face would show the big distinctions, but the body will show similarities to that of the happy-excited person, specifically, signs of increased animation.

All of that energy needs to go somewhere. If the person is in the presence of others and the cause of the excitement is open for public discussion, the person will want to share. She'll probably lock on to any keyword in the conversation that can steer it back to the subject of her excitement. If the cause of it is not open for discussion—an illicit affair at the office—she will leak her feelings when oblique references to the subject come up. Whether you can see the source of the excitement or not, you can easily see the aura caused by the bouncing energy. For this reason, few people can keep a secret that impacts their own lives.

Although the focus depends on what causes the excitement, it's almost always external; when excitement has an element of secretiveness, as in the case of an illicit affair, this focus will vacillate. If you put her source of excitement in the room, regardless of where her eyes are, her focus will be on that person. Even if the eyes move away, they will drag away. To anyone even mildly astute, it creates a stream of energy that signals "something's going on." The gossip columns call it "sparks flying." This is one reason why people know about an affair before the spouse who is being wronged. The focus is external, so the energy comes out.

Think of a child the first time she sees Santa—full of excitement, but conflicted about whether it's good or bad excitement. She knows he gives gifts, but that laugh sounds fake. Maybe he eats kids after he gives them gifts! After embracing a benevolent Santa, she imagines the possibilities of all he will give her; when she thinks of him later, her focus is internal. On Christmas night when she hears a sleigh bell ring, though, all of her energy turns externally to the old fat man in the red suit.

Interest

Energy high, direction sharp, focus external.

Back to the anger and joy profile. Full-blown curiosity can power the body as much as food. Think of an inquisitive toddler who cannot be distracted from tearing apart a new gift to see what's inside. Actually, that's a boy toddler; a girl with just as much interest in the gift is likely to explore its facets more cautiously and ask a lot of whys and hows. Regardless of the approach, all energy is directed at the object of their interest. *2001: A Space Odyssey* provides a perfect example of this in the opening scene in which the primates are obsessed with the obelisk. Any thought of self comes after "What the heck is this?" Or in the case of males, "Should I kill, eat, or breed this?"

In males, the predisposition toward action as part of satisfying curiosity keeps us externally focused, often without concept of self or personal limitations. As part of our people-watching for this book, we looked at young boys and girls on vacation with their parents in Estes Park, Colorado. This may not be a statistically valid assertion, but based on our observations, it sure is obvious: Little boys run on to things and into things and around things with reckless abandon. Little girls almost never do that. This is likely a response to high testosterone doses in the womb. Perhaps this natural inclination for action has served male primates well from an evolutionary point of view. The weaker male can pass his genes on to the object of his affection without regard for survival of the self if he acts more quickly. The alpha need not fear harm and can pass his genes without regard for personal injury. One has only to know a male child in his late teens to see this ape behavior in action.

Fear

Energy high, direction sharp, focus external.

If interest causes us to override our natural instincts to pull back, fear is the sudden reminder that we must do it. Fear arouses tremendous energy in preparation for action. When Greg was 8 years old, he was trick-or-treating with his 4-year-old brother, 6-year-old sister, and 3-year-old cousin. As they walked on to a porch, a man with a bloody stump for a head answered the door. Even a discerning 8-year-old did not recognize the stump as a pork chop sitting on top of a man's shirt. In total terror, he dove off the 3-foot-high porch and screamed to his little brother to run. The little brother was in the lead. Greg's sister, holding the hand of the toddler cousin, dragged him down the street while he screamed for her to run faster. In those days, Greg thought her hand wouldn't let go of him because it was paralyzed in fear. Today, the interpretation is that her action was a standard female response to terror: Save the baby.

Every one of those kids sharply directed all their energy at getting the hell out of there. That's how fear operates; whether or not the direction is ideal, it is aimed at something particular. The energy is typically balled up in fear awaiting a release command from the limbic brain to fight, flee, or freeze, or in the case of women, a combination of actions. In all of these cases, though, the energy is unidirectional and prepared, and the focus is external. The eyes dilate to take in as much data as possible about the source of the fear. Then the body either turns away from the source or toward the object to take a second look at the threat and determine a course of action. When the threat becomes omnipresent and overwhelming, a man takes action. This threshold for what is omnipresent varies from man to man.

However, a woman's external focus may be split between the threat and the object of her protection. For this reason, female prey will sometimes immediately attack a predator rather than run from it. These females don't want to leave their young as an appetizer, so they fight. In humans, the response is not as predictable, because females have a much better developed brain and a larger catalogue of options than her quadruped counterparts.

Secretiveness

Energy low, direction sharp, focus external.

When someone is trying to hide something, elements of the other moods will creep in. Is she excited because it is a surprise party? Afraid because it is an affair? Trying to hide the fact he is interested in something you are carrying or reading? In fact, you might see overlap in nearly all of the moods described here, primarily because secretiveness needs a root, emotional cause.

An attempt to be secretive is a conscious effort. As such, you have to keep energy low, stay directed, and maintain an external focus or you'll give yourself away. At the same time, most humans are not aware of the layers of moods they have, so maintaining absolute control over these elements is beyond most people's ability. In order to know what the person is hiding, you will have to work at uncovering the layers.

Here's an important irony that will help you: By its very nature, hiding something is energy intensive. Have you ever tried to keep a secret when someone is prodding? This energy is constantly trying to go somewhere, and as a consequence it tends to leak out in odd and visible ways. The more polished among us find successful routines to redirect this energy. Through experimentation, we learn what works, such as playing on our sexuality or even pretending to be dimwitted to divert suspicion from our real intent.

Secretiveness, therefore, is characterized by large amounts of contained energy. Look for adaptors, the movement of energy displacement. There is a direct relationship between the amount of energy someone is fighting to hold in or displace, and the significance of the secret.

When obsessed with a singular issue, a person has single direction; this is especially true with secretiveness. Everything in the person's mind revolves around the importance of covering tracks and preventing discovery. That plays out in clues. For example, just as a child obsessed with Santa turns every conversation to Santa, a secretly cheating spouse will take odd turns in conversation to reference or avoid reference to infidelity or the object of the infidelity. This can be sexual cheating or financial infidelity; that is, having a partner use joint funds without joint agreement. When referencing infidelity she is likely trying to test the water for how he feels about it or what he knows. When avoiding, she knows how he will react and wants to stay away at all costs from the topic. Either will create a contrived sort of division of the conversation. It reminds me of a story I heard from someone learning to drive a race car. The instructor said "Don't look at the wall or you'll hit it." So what do most people do? They look at the wall. It's just human nature.

Secretive people who are skillful maintain strict external focus. They want to stay away from too much of what is in their own heads—they don't want to hit the wall—and they want to focus on the other person's conversation. First of all, this allows him an opportunity to discover what the other knows and side-step discovery. People transmit their own thoughts when speaking, even when asking a question. Secondly, no one likes to keep a secret, so listening carefully might help him find a confidant.

An extreme version of this plays out in the interrogation rooms of police departments. When a person feeling guilty on some level is interrogated, and is hiding information, the suspect focuses so much on the questioner that he might project an unnatural friendliness. In effect, the suspect becomes charming. Greg describes a person like this as "glossy," and has codified the behavior after years of observation. In moving toward understanding *becoming a glossy image of self*, think of the synonyms for glossy, such as "shiny," "slick," and "smooth," and you can see what kind of image we're talking about. The suspect is so focused on staying away from what is inside his own head that he becomes hyper-focused, an active listener, and super attentive. These are superficial layers that are far beyond his norm.

Embarrassment

Energy low; direction sharp, focus internal.

Almost all grand embarrassment is preceded by secretiveness. This is not the momentary kind that comes from farting in public. Grand embarrassment can arise from displaced expectations all the way up to discovery of the family skeletons.

Embarrassed people typically do not know what to do with this sudden, unexpected flow of energy. They know what caused the embarrassment and sharply direct their attention on it. They don't know where to put all of the energy it provoked, though, so it often comes boomeranging back at them. Whether embarrassment becomes anger, excitement, joy, or confusion relates to how the person deals with directing the energy and whether the focus becomes internal or external. This will be largely culture-dependant.

Direction in embarrassment is unilateral. All arrows are lined with the course of action the person decides to take to escape the cause, even though displaced expectation makes the person seem distracted for a moment. An average American called to speak in front of a crowd will begin to use this direction of energy to create barriers and use adaptors to comfort him- or herself. This same person called a liar in public may have an extremely different, secondary reaction: one that includes discrediting the accuser. The course of action depends upon whether this highly directed energy is focused internally or externally.

Where a person focuses energy in embarrassment is largely cultural. When we say culture, we mean from micro-culture through super-culture. In May 1991, Queen Elizabeth paid a visit to the Marshall Heights Community Development Organization, a subsidized housing project in Washington, D.C. Resident Alice Frazier greeted Her Majesty with a bear hug, which caused a mixture of abject embarrassment and shock on the part of former First Lady Barbara Bush, the Mayor of Washington, D.C., and the Secretary of Housing and Urban Development. In fact, the only people who didn't seem to be bothered by the egregious breach of protocol were Mrs. Frazier and the Queen.

The more comfortable a person is with an experience, no matter how unusual, the more likely a person will handle the embarrassing moment tactfully, gracefully, and internalize the energy.

Experiment with this system (which Greg developed, but you should now personalize) of codifying the three main traits of human moods. Make your own table and create profiles for other emotional states as well, for honing your "review" skills. Put other moods on the list, pay attention, and categorize the three elements of those moods.

Expand the system and make it your own. What other criteria might you add? How about dress? Is it even possible for the Pope to show absolute joy—an explosion of energy—while he's wearing his mitre and pallium, and carrying the pastoral staff? This is not only a matter of the physical limitations of the clothing, but also the gravity of the office represented by the clothing.

Does the role you play in life impact your expressions of moods? Surely the Queen would have reacted differently to the hugger if she were not practiced in controlling her state. Is there likely a difference in energy level and focus as we shift from role to role in our daily lives? Most humans have a thick, layered skin of diversions and disguises when it comes to emotions; this system is just one more way to skin the monkey.

Posture

Culture profoundly affects posture. From the smallest group to the largest, you need to consider influences on openness, energy, flexibility, and movements, which are all elements of posture. This gives you the basic model for how we will analyze posture to further develop your holistic view of body language. Each of these will play a part in what the person is conveying, intentionally or unintentionally, and each will reflect cultural influences.

What passes for good posture among average Americans would cause swift and severe punishment for any member of United States Marine Corps. When Greg began his military career, he was a short, 14-year-old junior ROTC (Reserve Officers' Training Corps) student. He was cajoled, ridiculed, and taught to stand like a soldier before most people ever consider joining the Army. Prepared for basic training and skilled in drills and ceremony, he felt ready for the rest of his Army career—at least the marching part. Five years later, the Army surprised him with an assignment to The Old Guard. Among other things, The Old Guard protects the Tomb of the Unknowns at Arlington National Cemetery and has a prominent role in burials at the cemetery. Greg soon realized his existing idea of good military posture fell short of the standards achieved by seasoned members of The Old Guard. Years later while serving in the military intelligence unit, a Major commented that he could tell Greg had been an Old Guard member by his ladder-straight back. The Old Guard micro-culture and the military intelligence micro-culture that is had very different takes on "military posture." The Old-Guard standard remains so much a ruling element in Greg's musculoskeletal presentation that it is evident even now. While working in international business recently, a psychologist hired by his company to do training remarked that Greg stands like a soldier.

During a night guard shift during Operation Desert Storm, he saw the effect of U.S. military culture starkly. With night-vision goggles, the world takes on a green glow that allows a person to see detail relatively well up close, but poorly at a distance. Looking through them, Greg saw how easy it was to pick an American by posture. The good news is that the erect posture projected discipline and focus. The bad news is that it potentially made the Iraqi snipers' target acquisition much easier.

Openness

Let's look at "closed" before "open" to engender your perspective on the topic.

When you started reading this book one of your suppositions was likely that crossed arms served as a defense, or meant that someone wanted to close you out. Did someone tell you that's what it meant, or did you feel it? Crossed arms are, in fact, one way that a person can block you out, but it can also signal fear, cold, confidence, arrogance, hiding a fat belly, and much more depending on context. Look for whether the hands are comfortably tucked underneath the arms that are crossed, or displayed in a more aggressive or negative posture.

Other ways of blocking include closing the elbows to the side (stock-in-trade for Donald Trump), tightly buttoned clothing, barricading oneself behind a holy symbol such as a cross, and turning to oblique angles. Americans typically think that facing a person straight on while talking signifies honesty. Ironically, given a choice, two American men will probably not sit directly facing each other. Most will choose to sit at oblique angles. It is a subconscious way that men convey they do not wish to engage in confrontation. If you think in terms of apes again, facing directly into the eyes of the alpha will likely result, at the very least, in a demonstration of dominance. So, is this natural preference to sit at an angle an echo of the ape in us? Think of the last time you saw two American men in an altercation. Inevitably, the two square off, face-to-face; the implication is that the angled posture is much friendlier. In contrast to this, it is not unusual to see two Arab men nearly touching faces and square-on discussing details of their weekend plans. If you're a man, take a minute and think about your own posture *vis-a-vis* other men of your own culture. If you're a woman, think about how you convey openness. It's generally in the same way that men display confrontation—face-to-face.

As an exercise for what you just learned, look in the mirror. Place your elbows close to your sides and raise your palms as if you are helpless. Now do the same gesture, but raise the elbows from the body. Which seems protected? Which seems genuine? Traditionally, open arms are viewed as welcome. This closed-to-the-sides posture showing vulnerability is instinctively distrusted by every one of our students. Most cannot tell you why.

Our nature is to demonstrate how open we are to acquaintances, whether new or old. "Warm" and "open" take on different appearances in different cultures, but all have one thing in common: displaying vulnerability to show openness.

The military salute is the most formal of greetings, a way to show servitude to superiors. A rigid and formalized gesture, it presents the right hand to the brow. Numerous theories try to explain why this developed, from a knight opening his visor to show his face, to the exposure of a hand without a weapon. The meaning is still the same: "I am raising my primary weapon into a non-ready position, to show servitude."

The American handshake carries a related meaning: I am offering you my primary weapon and I would like yours in exchange. The Asian bow conveys "I am lowering my unprotected skull." How much more open, that is, vulnerable, can a human get? These actions capture the essence of why openness is so important in communication. Humans are a perceptive lot even when their culture dulls the senses.

Openness can come from a relative position as well. If a man stands at a somewhat oblique angle to another American man, he will perceive it as open. If he turns to face him head on, you usually notice he will shift to keep this position less confrontational. By oblique we do not mean a T-formation. If you do move to the T and close in on the person's dominant hand, he will perceive that as a threat, too. Try it if you doubt this. Add to that squared shoulders as you talk. Do you see a difference? Experiment with someone you know, not someone you've just met in an elevator.

Clothing can demonstrate openness as well. When John Mark Karr confessed to killing JonBenét Ramsey, the child beauty queen, he wore his collar buttoned to the top. Oddly enough, the first question thrown at Greg on CNN that night related to his tightly buttoned collar. This is a piece of body language that probably strikes many people as closed at first glance. Greg avoided the question, by the way, because he did not know whether it was his norm; we do not like to think in absolutes and did not want to be painted into that corner. Karr's micro-culture could play a part in his dressing that way. But if that is not his norm, buttoning his collar to the top is, in fact, a barrier.

Openness, or lack thereof, can also be demonstrated by barriering with objects or with natural tools: hands, ankles, knees, or even fingers. Objects, such as a rolled magazine, purse, laser pointer, or a cell phone, can make a person feel safer. Look for use of these tools not as a screen to hide body language physically, but as a way to divert energy away from the face and body, much like a fan dancer in a burlesque show. Repeated or consistent use of them as barriers in a conversation probably means you should look beyond them to find nervousness, anger, disgust, or embarrassment. In an office, of course, the most common barrier is a person's desk.

In class, we both flash pictures of several people on the screen, and after a split second, ask: "Who do you trust?" Inevitably, the person they trust least is the one who looks the most closed. Whether it is because of dress that is traditionally non-Western, or clothes that cover more of the person than most Americans are accustomed to seeing, the formula becomes "The more hidden, the less trustworthy." Would growing up in Saudi Arabia change this? It is highly likely.

Where your put your hands and how closed you sit or stand will impact how trusted you are. Years ago, when Greg was interviewing for a job he wasn't particularly interested in, he intentionally modified his posture during the interview to see how the interviewer would react. The more he rounded his upper body and hid his hands—closed signs that represent vulnerability—the more probing the interviewer became.

Energy

Energy level tells more about what is going on in the head than the body.

Maryann did a couple of 10-day, multi-sport adventure races, which were producer Mark Burnett's precursors to the *Survivor* reality television series. Teams were eliminated if they didn't make it to a checkpoint on time, and making it to checkpoints generally meant going without sleep, or taking no more than a nap. But even after days with very little sleep, the teams that finished the race continued to be hard-charging. Maryann interviewed a number of the participants for her book on the success secrets of extreme athletes and, uniformly, the competitors who finished the race credited the spirit of their teammates, the breathtaking scenery, and other psychological factors with sustaining their energy.

How well do you sleep the night before a big trip? How about the night before the first day of a new job? This energy affects posture more than facial expression. You can look like hell in the face from lack of sleep, but move around as though you are yourself and you will appear to be fine.

The energy we talking about here is not the bubbly little kid kind, which I do cover in the section on movement. This is energy to the joints that gives you the impression the person's back is strong and under control versus sloppy and sagging. Depression and a sense of failure manifest themselves in lack of energy to the joints. The back is similar to a suspension bridge and all of those cables need energy to stay taut. When the energy subsides, the posture droops.

As you learn about baselining in Chapter 7, you will see how important this criterion becomes in reading an individual's body language. Even if a person's normal posture is not up to Old Guard standards, you can tell when his energy level changes, and move toward conclusions about his emotional and mental state.

Flexibility

Any personal trainer or physical therapist will harp on the benefits of flexibility, but the definition here is a little different from theirs. By flexibility we refer to rounded movements—swivels, slumps, bends at the joints, and so on—as opposed to movements with a degree of rigidity. Posture with square corners—shoulders back, feet planted firmly beneath—is a more male, and less flexible, posture. Rounded shoulders and feet that shift weight from one side to another is typically more female and seen as feminine. The gender differences between these postures come out of anatomical differences, which also tend to make women more flexible in the conventional sense used by trainers and therapists.

Men typically have broader, more developed shoulders, and a narrower pelvis with legs closely set. This creates an image that is triangular and has harsher angles than a woman's body. The angles translate to straighter movement and a squarer gait. Men walk and move in a straight line very efficiently. This squared-off movement will often give away even the well-practiced transgender females and drag queens who don't have a woman's broad-set hips and their natural predisposition toward lateral, fluid movement. Movement of men's arms looks as though it originates from above, but when a woman moves her arms, it's not as if it is dangling as much as it is sweeping from below. Add to this the fact that muscles attach at different points on the frame and you get a naturally more rounded look in women than men. Sure, this can be disguised, hidden, or changed with clothing, weight, surgery, exercise, or training, but no matter how you slice it, all these elements do is decorate the frame, not alter it.

As a reminder, this discussion is not about men and women having equal competence in certain sports and other physical challenges. These distinctions are only important in discussing posture as it relates to body language.

With gender being a shifting concept in our culture, we want to make one quick note here: Anger will move you closer to the behavior of the gender you identify with. Women will instinctively express their femininity, rounding the shoulders and shifting the center of gravity. Very effeminate men will become more demonstratively feminine. Men and more masculine women will make themselves squarer and blocky in their movement. When people become enraged the animal takes over, and you can see if the gender identity they usually project is an act. If it's not tied to the person's sense of being, the ape will take over and gender will disappear. The part of our brains tied to "pretending" is removed when we get to the ape side.

Regardless of how hard-coded that identity might be, the structure the identity is built over has an impact. Look at Caitlyn Jenner. Although makeup, surgery, and a tasteful wardrobe make her image more feminine than masculine, Caitlyn is dealing with lot of well-developed tendon and muscle connection, with years of testosterone flowing that inform her body's reactions. Regardless of what and how the personality thinks it is moving, there are still huge masculine residuals in Caitlyn. When she wiped away tears during her acceptance of the Arthur Ashe Courage Award at the 2015 ESPYs, Caitlyn used the knuckle of her index finger, which is distinctly a male movement.

Men rub; women stroke. Yes, it is a learned behavior, but also impacted by physiology.

One constant is that when people become emotionally tender, all of us become more rounded. Go to a bar, or any place you can watch people trying to make a connection. In a bar, the men will be very masculine, square standing, and using straight-line movement until they pass a certain point, at which bonding begins. At that moment, the speed of behavior slows and the man's movement and posture will start to round. The same is true for sadness and depression. Watch men around you become softer as these emotions hit.

Movement

Every subculture of which you are a part will affect how you move. Professional dancers will show traces of training in daily movement. Police officers responsible for crowd control will also have residual movement patterns. Everything we do, whether as a hobby or profession, leaves muscle memory on our bodies. In this section, we give you an overview of movement. An entire book could be dedicated to reading the body language of movement and ritual, so consider this simply an introduction to gait, center of gravity, and overall body movement.

Gait

"Put some pep in your step" is a military expression that actually means something specific. Drill sergeants will use this cliché when trying to turn average Americans into marching soldiers. The normal marching gait is called quick-time. A cadence of 120 steps per minute, a stride of 30 inches heel to toe, and arm movement of 9 inches to the front and 6 inches to the rear is the prescribed gait for an American soldier while marching. A drill instructor drums the proper lilt, or spring, to the military marching step into your head with "stop bee-bopping" or some other cliché to remind you that marching leaves no room for creativity. Just do what you are told by the person calling the commands. When we say that culture has a pronounced impact on gait, think about marching like that almost every day for 15 years and you have the most extreme example we can think of. Muscle memory from that repeated experience will forever change the way you walk.

Let's use these components to analyze the different elements of gait: speed, stride, lilt, and focus.

Speed

Speed correlates to a sense of urgency. It's funny to see a man who has never run a day in his life struggling to make his way at high-speed through the airport. Maybe airport security should have a "lumbering ape" alert so people can drag their children to safety. The running man who "never" runs has no muscle memory to support that speed, so even without a baseline, you can determine with certainty that his emotional state is "urgency." Although speed can be achieved by simply lengthening the stride, most people do not have the option of lengthening stride enough to fulfill this sense of urgency. Contrast this with runners moving through the airport. If they run on a regular basis they would rarely get a second glance because there is a congruity between pace and muscle memory.

Stride

Most people have a natural stride or length of step that falls somewhere around the 30-inch range (heel to toe) that the Army dictated for marching. Height and length of limbs dictate this, of course, as well as travel companions.

With a 36-inch inseam and wearing boots, Greg has long legs; Maryann doesn't. When we launched *How to Spot a Liar* at The Capitol in Washington, D.C., we were asked to meet with a news team from Channel 9. A little confusion about the exact location sent us several blocks away from the actual rendezvous point. When we called and found out we needed to travel several blocks, Greg did not change his speed, but simply lengthened his stride to what is normal for him. Maryann had no more length in her stride, so her only option was to speed; in fact, every five to seven steps she would jog a few steps in her heels. It's a fond memory because it added texture to the day (and her heels no doubt added texture to the grounds on the West Lawn of the Capitol).

This shortening or lengthening of stride will tell you a bit about the urgency and intent of the person in the situation. In this case, the urgency and intent were clear. Maryann and Greg were carrying on a civil conversation, so why would Greg walk Maryann into the ground unless we were in a hurry to get somewhere? Change the picture a bit. What if we were both walking the same pace, but Maryann was complaining about something he had done? The message of Greg's body language then changes to "I'm getting away from you."

Lilt

A man headed for the gas chamber is not likely to do so with a spring in his step. The opposite is true when someone is walking on stage for well-deserved recognition. Even an introvert will telegraph his thoughts with a bounce in his step when being recognized for brilliance.

Focus

Have you ever been behind (or maybe you are part of) an old couple in an automobile just watching the cows eat grass? Then you know where we are going with the focus piece.

Let's go back to the airport, where you can spot the people who do not travel often. The trip is the adventure, not the destination. They clog the moving sidewalks, miss moving up in line when it's their turn, and just generally do not seem to notice what is going on around them. The reason is focus. The seasoned traveler sees the security line, airport, and check-in as hindrances to his eventual goal. He is going somewhere to do something and the result is a focus of movement.

Center of Gravity

Personal trainers and physical therapists have a specific physiological meaning for "center of gravity." Greg has his own definition. He uses the phrase to mean the center of a person's movement, where the energy is focused. Elements such as gender, weight, and culture play into this and simple observation will enable you to recognize it, too.

When was the last time you saw a young man wandering aimlessly and looking unhappy? Though thin and light on his feet, his energy has sunken to a point well below his face. An expression such as "down in the dumps" captures his look. Men who walk solidly and land squarely on the heels of their feet appear grounded. Higher, more expressive energy centered around the upper body appears more feminine. The expression "light in the loafers" to describe an effeminate male refers to this look. All of these points of focus for energy play into my view of the person's center of gravity.

A young American man will typically have a center of gravity that is high and somewhere around the chest. Contrast this to an American woman who will have a center of gravity somewhat lower—typically between solar plexus and hips. Gymnastics equipment and events are one example in which center of gravity plays a key role in the design: Men do parallel bars and rings to take advantage of upper body strength; women do uneven parallel bars and balance beam to exploit the athletic advantages of their lower center of gravity. This affects walking and other common movements in a number of ways.

As a typical American man moves, he will catch his weight on his heels and roll forward to the balls of his feet. His shoulders are the eye-catching part of his movement; his hips are typically squared. When an American woman walks, she is likely to catch her weight somewhere forward of the heel; many women actually walk on the balls of their feet. Her hips are the eye-catching part of her movement. Although she may pose her shoulders due to good posture or to give a better look at her assets, those gestures reflect intention, not an anatomical predisposition.

Let's use this information for an exercise. If you are a woman: Walk with your shoulders squared and land on your heels; roll your weight to the balls of your feet with your hips square and no swish. How does that feel? Even if you think yourself a bit masculine, the movements are likely uncomfortable physically, because your hips are poorly placed on the pelvis for this movement. Did you notice how little you use your shoulders? Now watch other women try this and contrast it with what you see in men. If you are a man: Raise the weight from your heels and move it forward to the center or balls of your feet. Lead with your hips and slightly sway as you walk. Try not to engage your shoulders in a swagger. (I have made the men's test easier because their brains work better with finite tasks.) What did you find? Does the term "light in the loafers" come to mind?

As we age and add weight, the center of gravity usually heads south. Nature takes away the squareness of most men through muscle atrophy and padding at the mid-section. An old Southernism calls this "furniture disease"—when your chest falls into your drawers. Men start to lose muscle mass in the chest and shoulders; what you get is a shrunken, droopy upper body, thickened waist, and flabby behind. Oh, but chances are good he walks the same—heel-toe-heel-toe—because of his muscle memory. Now, however, the extra weight on his frame striking the heels jars his compressing spine, so he shifts forward off the heel. The once tall-standing, high-center-of-gravity man now pitches forward when he walks. His square posture is more rounded and he looks centered closer to the solar plexus or hips. His gait and appearance has become more feminine with age. Reading the posture portion of his body language must take this into consideration. With many older men, you will need to pay attention to how they compensate for the changes.

Take Robert Duvall, for instance. How does he maintain his image of a masculine man even at the age of 85? Did his weight shift to his drawers? If you look at him in *Apocalypse Now* (1979) and again in *Jack Reacher* (2012), he did become a different kind of manly man. He's Lieutenant Colonel Bill Kilgore, the commander of a cavalry squadron who calls in napalm sorties in Vietnam in the earlier movie, and a crusty, gun-toting geezer in *Jack Reacher*. And you still wouldn't want to mess with either version of his manliness. He has a uniquely masculine gait due to his extreme bow-leggedness; age can't diminish it, short of losing his ability to walk. He overcomes age by thoroughly engaging with the audience, squaring his shoulders, thrusting his jaw, and making just a few, decisive hand and arm movements.

Knowing what you know now, however, go back and watch *Apocalypse Now* and *Jack Reacher* and compare Duvall's center of gravity in them. Is age the only thing that changes our center of gravity?

Let's try a couple more exercises with the information you've learned so far. First, walk along at you normal gait and pace. Now remember the last deeply emotional experience you had. A good chewing from the boss? A disappointing date? Failing a test? Pay attention to your center of gravity. Your head likely went down and to the right in response to emotion. When you carry around 20 pounds of dead weight in the form of your head and change its position relative to the body, everything has to accommodate it. It is simple mechanics.

Second, sadness and the darker emotions will drop your center of gravity and instantly age your movement, but lighter emotions will raise your center of gravity. Hold back on something exciting you want to share with someone until the last possible minute. Tune into your own body language as you move toward that person physically, with the intent of connecting with him emotionally. If you are middle-aged or older, you will feel youth come back to your body as your exuberance causes you to pick up your step and move more nimbly to get there.

Overall Movement

Is boundless activity or serenity more associated with the "ideal" in your culture? Do you want your children to bounce around and climb things, or to learn quickly to control and focus their energy?

In the United States, when a man enters a room, he will be perceived as in control and powerful if he is calm. There is a caveat: If he stands for too long with no contact with others, he becomes an outsider. Low levels of movement, with hands controlled and decisive at or around waist-level, are viewed as masculine in our northern European-descended culture. This same level of inactivity may be seen as odd coming from a woman.

Contrast this behavior with those of Mediterranean and Latin descent in the United States—Italians, Hispanics, Greeks, Turks, and so on. These cultures all use the hands demonstratively as part of normal illustration. The elbows may even rise close to shoulder level in men of these cultures. People with an Anglo-centric background may see this kind of gesturing as hot-tempered, too emotionally involved. Let's get some perspective on this, though: Germanics and Brits are more the exception to body language than the norm in humankind. The waist-high, controlled gestures probably seem rather lame and uncommitted to many people around the world.

Overall movement is affected by several factors: some biological, some cultural, and some part of micro-culture so obscure that one can only wonder where they come from. We all know kids with a tremendous amount of energy and that energy needs to go somewhere. They flit about and border on what could be called hyperactive. Even after years of "be still" and "sit down," they have energy that leaks out of their hands, their feet, and their mouths. Those aren't signs that a kid necessarily needs to be medicated; maybe his mom and dad were like that, too.

In reading overall movement, look for energy that is contained and leaking from somewhere else. The scene in *The Bird Cage* in which Robin Williams tries to contain his flamboyant partner's behavior by putting him in a suit and teaching him to "walk like a man" provides an extreme example of that.

Application

We could easily have started this book with the holistic chapter, but that would have skewed your vision of the smaller, more subtle signals people send. Rather than that quick-fix approach to reading body language, you have to develop an eye for reviewing the pieces of body language and speculating about what they could mean. You have practiced your review skills to the point that you can now see similarities and differences. And you understand that sometimesa person scratches his or her nose because it itches.

Using the holistic approach with those basics to better understand the overall person now allows you to create categories of moods. The large-chunk pieces allow you to overlay the smaller, subtler actions you've examined and to notice what stands out. When your eyes notice a nuance that has more meaning than the collection of individual actions, you are using the "E" in R.E.A.D.

For example, you have a project that is falling behind, but manage to keep your fingers in the dam to prevent catastrophe. You watch the boss come in Friday morning. He walks intently, his gait faster than normal. As he approaches the office, he is holding his coffee with both hands and only releases to rub his forehead once. His overall movement is contained, but there is a nervous energy; it is choppier than normal. As he passes your door, he glances at his shoes. Should you be concerned? If so, why? Nothing occurs in a vacuum, so ask yourself what real-life elements would play in here. Paranoid delusions aside, you might evaluate the situation like this:

- The faster-than-normal gait with barriering projects a desire to minimize exposure time.
- The jerky movement indicates a preoccupied mind.
- The fact that he averted his gaze down could be outright guilt.

Your interpretation at this point is that maybe you should be concerned. After all, Friday in the United States is the most popular day to terminate employees for non-performance. What you have done in this situation is review all of the body language and apply what you know about the boss's norms, and then look for the pieces that stand out to evaluate his body language. You added to that a factor that colors the context—something we will go into more in Chapter 7.

Up until now, we've given you overall tools for absorbing information about other people. We didn't have to teach you to evaluate—you taught yourself the "E." You are now noticing the subtleties of a person's communication style and are almost ready to move on. Almost. First, you need to know what causes this information to be tainted. It is time to start working on your filters.

6

Filters: Sex and Other Misconceptions

You have collected and cataloged input (R) and overlaid some basic rules about humans on to what is "normal" (E), and now it's time move to analysis (A), by first identifying and then removing your blinders, or filters.

If you spent the first 20 years of your life in Philadelphia, Pennsylvania, with no heavy ethnic orientation, it's possible to make certain assumptions about your body language. The kind of movements you make will be somewhat at odds with what is normal and acceptable for someone from the backwoods of Georgia. The cadence of your speech, word choices, and other aspects of your verbal, vocal, and non-verbal communication will also help build a profile.

Here's a quirky example of how that verbal and non-verbal come together to indicate where you're from: American Sign Language executed by someone from Philadelphia may have a heavy regional accent. A signer from another part of the country might be able sign back, "Hey, you're from Philadelphia!"[1]

When you offer an observation like that, it suggests to the other person that you may know more about her than just where she's from. Why? You're attentive and come across as well-informed—at least about something. A palm reader without any special powers, except the knowledge of communication filters, will also be able to suggest that she knows more about you than she actually does. You walk away $100 poorer, convinced that she saw into your past, therefore she must know something about your future.

Your ability to read someone else's body language depends on your knowledge of how you filter information and what filters other people are bringing to the encounter. If you're the boy from the backwoods of Georgia who meets that city gal from Philadelphia, you might interpret normal, friendly body language as pushy or insincere simply because she isn't communicating with her arms and face the way women in your hometown do. And if you're the fortune teller, you are preying on the filters the customer has that make her see only what she wants to see. Assumptions, projections, and biases can clog your ability to sense and intuit information about someone.

By applying R.E.A.D., you will become better than the pieces of information in this book. That is, you will be equipped to take this system and expand it by integrating your knowledge to create a one-of-a-kind understanding of body language, signaling, and communication.

There is a flip side to this. Sometimes we can go too far in applying our assumptions, and that creates filters to our ability to read people. Here is a scenario that clarifies the point: As entertainment for a meeting in New Orleans, the host organization hired an authentic-looking fortune teller. Greg decided to scout her out and see what kind of tricks she was using. He watched as a man of about 50 said to his wife, "This should be fun, honey!" and sat down with the young woman, who began turning over her cards. The man said he always enjoyed a good reading and told her he had a good friend who did this professionally. A look of "uh oh" came over the fortune teller's face. She took another look at him, and his wife, and jumped to a conclusion about their circumstances—ostensibly by reading the cards: "I see your family is all doing great." The man and his wife looked at each other with intense sadness. The man rose from the table and hugged his wife as they walked away. I learned that they had just lost their teenage daughter to cancer. This card reader had projected too far, blinding herself to body language and details by assuming it would be a safe bet to talk about family, because most of the turmoil of children and family has subsided for men in their 50s.

Gender

Men and women can more easily understand each other than act like each other. That said, understanding each other is far from easy. The biological and anatomical differences that influence behavior also switch on powerful filters that make it hard for us to eliminate biases we have about the other sex. In considering those differences, center your attention on both—why gender-related filters have such control over our thinking and how they operate, and how men and women differ in their body language.

We want to insert something here about gender identity that has nothing to do with political correctness, but everything to do with the latest information in the fields of neuroscience and anatomy. The gender you appear to be is not always a clear designation of the gender you identify with. We're not necessarily talking about people who want to undergo a transition to the other gender, although they are part of the discussion. We are primarily talking about people like "Jeff," who is happily married and who speaks and writes often about women's issues, the negative impact on society of the "alpha male," and the need for female leadership. His body language is softer than what is normally associated with a man, and he's stereotypically female in his writing and speech in that he gravitates toward subtlety and making a point more indirectly than typical male counterparts.

The word *typical* is important here because our discussion of gender is focused on what is typical. An article entitled "Gender Patterns in Talking" in *WomanPilot* magazine captured the essence of our approach well: "When looking at gender patterns in talking, we need to remember that people view their ways of talking as a natural behavior. So our speech patterns are basically automatic. Women and men as a group talk in particular ways. The fact that individuals do not fit the pattern doesn't make the pattern not typical."[2]

Immediately following that piece of information, the authors noted: "Research tell us that communication styles of men and women differ dramatically." So, yes, there are women who have more traditionally male communication and behavior patterns, and vice versa. Simple observation bears out that fact. That does not negate the fact that we can learn a great deal from typical patterns.

Men's communication style often mimics their thinking style. Make a plan and stick to it. Women's communication style tends to be more of a negotiation, a back-and-forth interaction. Both can be altered by training, whether formal or informal and operant conditioning.

With that in mind, our discussion starts with the impact of the primary sex organs, which do not just affect how we see our identity, but they also affect how we think, move, and live. This is mainly through the introduction of hormones to our systems, which starts in the womb. Whether we want to admit it or not, we all start as female. If doses of testosterone later flood the fetus, the tissue that would have become an ovary can descend to become a testicle. Some researchers have documented that the length of man's or woman's ring finger in comparison to the index finger will tell you how much testosterone a person was exposed to as a fetus. People with longer ring fingers theoretically were exposed to more testosterone in the womb than others.[3]

Years ago, before the high risks in Greg's life were re-organizing companies, a female interrogator who worked with Greg once told him that he suffered from testosterone poisoning because of his risk model. The implications are clear. Whether you measure it in broken bones or the cost of car insurance, testosterone drives young males to take more physical risks than young females. Jim McCormick, whose expertise as a speaker, author, and coach is "intelligent risk-taking," conducted a study related to the risk inclination of various populations:

> My research shows that men's and women's inclination to take social and creative risks are essentially identical. The greatest difference in risk inclination between men and women is in physical risks, with men noticeably more comfortable with physical risks.
>
> The two types of risks for which women indicate a greater risk inclination than men are relationship risks and emotional risks. Of note is that women's general risk inclination increases for many women once they are beyond childbearing age.[4]

As Jim's data highlights, young women are less likely to take physical risks, but consider an underlying logic for this: It's in a woman's nature to protect the egg. An ovary typically produces and releases one egg per month; a female is born with every egg she will ever have. Given the premise that human beings are first and foremost designed for preservation of species, it is logical to assert that the egg is precious and the body gives us the instinct to protect it. We want to forget how important instinct is to us because it reminds us we are shaved apes. Males, on the other hand, produce sperm on a daily basis so there is no need to stockpile. One man can fertilize dozens of women easily. Men, unlike most women, are quite satisfied with taking risks if it gets them an immediate reward.

Men are expendable in the "survival of species" equation. And as a result, they compete fiercely for the validation of women. The chest pounding of our primate cousins shows through in young men with high risk-taking and accomplishments of some kind replacing alpha-ape challenges like charging and chest pounding. It often continues well past a man's 20s, as we know!

For *Going Ape: The Alpha Male*, National Geographic recruited Greg—whom they designated the "alpha expert"—to create an experiment that demonstrated the alpha behavior in men. The "contestants" were told they were going to be on a reality show to rebuild a car for a donor and show their teamwork. The truth was more insidious. Through hidden cameras, Greg and the primatologists had the opportunity to watch the men interact with each other, deal with an attractive young woman, create a group and a plan, and work on the vehicle. In the end, as they were engaged in rebuilding the car, Greg was sent in to arouse alpha male behavior. The behaviors, only some of which were shown in the broadcast, were stereotypical men posing and one-upping each other for the attention of the young woman. They did things like move between her and other men and attempt to isolate her from the group. Also, each man felt the need to tell her how great he was at something. In the end, the role Greg played was to push buttons. The alpha who emerged built coalition with the other males to protect them from the threat posed by a bellicose Greg. Demonstrating the use of a thinking brain even in the presence of all that "testosterone poisoning," the alpha protected "his" resources.

This behavior shows in prominent displays of "plumage ruffling" among men as they compete for validation by the opposite sex even when there is no breeding opportunity. It might involve grooming, toys, accomplishments, or just about any other thing a male brain can think of. Interestingly, once a man is perceived as alpha his "flexing" stops and others around him become more pronounced.

The next consideration in terms of behavior is that breeding for a female mammal is only the beginning of a relationship. She faces weeks, months, or even years of nurturing after that. Women are designed for nurturing. In contrast, breeding is a finite task for males: attract, breed, sleep. We can make elaborate plans to get to that end, but the end is just that. Without social constraints, males would not insert themselves in the nurturing the process. With social constraints—humans enjoy making life more complicated—males stay involved and help preserve culture.

If we assume, then, that breeding is a finite task for males and the beginning of a process for females, we can see there will be differences in the way we approach nearly everything. The long-term impact is that even when women of childbearing age are afraid, there is a part of them that instinctively protects the Holy Grail of the species: the egg. This behavior is all part of normal thinking and reactions, according to neuropsychiatrist and author Louann Brizenden. "The mommy-brain transformation gets underway at conception and can take over even the most career-oriented woman's circuits, changing the way she thinks, feels, and what she finds important."[5]

Step back several thousand years and look at the behavior patterns of our primitive ancestors. Males were the hunters out of necessity, not only because of their physique, but also because the females were either pregnant or tending to the young. The male brain is also better suited to this type of finite-task thinking. They make wonderful long-range plans and stick to them. On the flip-side, they are not quite as good at making a flexible plan and constantly tweaking it to get a long-term result. Our male ancestors would have said, "There is this animal who is always here at this time. Let us go kill it." The females would say "Somewhere out there are some really good berries. I am not sure where they are, but they will be good with meat so let us go find them." This evolved into "These berries are really good. Let's make sure that bush stays alive." Does that sound familiar? Is it any wonder that, through cooperation, the male and female brain came up with agriculture? The male brain probably conquered the plant by moving it; the female kept it alive. Granted, this is a simplistic look at male and female brains, but the concept does play out in our interaction.

The impact of testosterone on our modern, highly developed brains should not be underestimated. Male brains do not develop the corpus callosum into the same shape and size as is generally found in female brains and scientists from the University of California at Los Angeles concluded "These anatomical sex differences could, in part, underlie gender-related differences in behavior."[6] Scientists think this difference makes the female brain manage communication from left to right more efficiently. The result is what women see as the one-trick-pony male mind. A woman will see many sides of the same equation as she looks for how to "nurture" the problem and create a solution. Another effect is that women are hyper-communicators and do so with many more words and much more nuance to body language.

Males tend to have clarity of focus on a single finite task, and as part of that focus, typically don't have high-speed, vibrant interaction between the left and right brains. When a female observes that plodding process and asks, "Why didn't you...?" and "What if...?" one thought immediately enters the male mind: "Why can't you think in a logical progressive fashion: A,B,C?" This difference in thinking makes the male mind think the female mind is flighty, when, in fact, she's processing creatively and logically in rapid succession. If men do not ask for directions, it is because they have a plan and they know that it is right from the beginning.

Just as the human skeleton dictates movement, the reproductive system plays its part in human behaviors and movements as well. This is never more visible than in children in the throes of puberty. A perfectly sane male child at 12 years old has lost his mind by 16. Suddenly, his brain has become more decidedly male and, as part of the process, is being outvoted two to one.

Prior to serving as an interrogator, Greg was with The Old Guard, the oldest active duty regiment in the U.S. Army and the one assigned to conduct memorial services and ceremonies. They had an obvious need to project discipline and fitness. At one point, their commander brought in a young female Marine who taught aerobics. Aside from being attractive and dressed in spandex, that infantry unit quickly concluded she had no value to them. Testosterone filled the air as they scoffed at doing aerobics. The commander informed them that they could add old bowling pins to the routine, because he'd acquired them from the newly rehabbed alley. They muttered things to each other about looking like gay clowns. This macho attitude lasted for about 10 minutes until this ultra-fit tiny blonde woman worked their asses into the ground. She told them in the beginning to use only one pin, but, of course, they used more than that. The men quickly hit muscle failure.

The story illustrates this point: Men and women move very differently. Although the men in the unit made very large square movements in order to remain masculine, the instructor and the men who didn't care about being macho made soft sweeping movements that used the energy of the swinging pins, instead of trying to control them.

The very nature of male movement is reflected in every part of our body language. When a man acts more like a woman, you will likely see superficial signs of female movement patterns, but the skeleton will anchor the movement in maleness. With the physical and innately-related mental gender differences in mind, let's take a look at some basics of human communication. A good starting point is the gestures touched on in Chapter 3—adaptors, barriers, and illustrators.

Now you have some basic knowledge that will help strip away filters and look at what you have seen already. Do gender and the gender role affect what you have seen—enough to change your mind about some conclusions you've jumped to? If there are men vying for alpha status, does it impact rigidity of body? Is that annoyance you thought you saw between a man and woman really annoyance, or is it simply frustration from wondering why she just doesn't get the simplicity of the plan, and why he hasn't thought of all the details?

Adaptors

One of the most powerful differences between men and women is in the use of adaptors. We use the word *powerful* intentionally. Men are tactile creatures who prefer to overdo everything. If one nail is good, two are better. Comedians have made careers around this.

As noted previously, adaptors are nothing more than the body finding a way to comfort itself in a foreign or stressful situation; it's creating familiar in the unfamiliar. Think of a coyote pacing in a cage. A man waiting outside the delivery room will likely look very much like the coyote. What do you think is going on in the coyote's head? Is it any different from what is going through the expectant father's head? Maybe the actual content differs, but the process is the same: obsession with one thing. When the brain obsesses, the body takes over.

In terms of using adaptors, the male tendency toward the tactile means that men will transfer more physical energy than women. A man will rub his eyes hard in response to stress, whereas a woman will stroke lightly beneath the eyes, almost in petting fashion. A common assumption is that women don't want to smear their makeup, but you will see this type of touching in cultures where women don't wear eye makeup. It is as if the nurturing piece of femininity even transfers to the self.

A woman who is uncomfortable will place the fingers of one hand in the palm of the other, thereby creating not only an adaptor as she lightly massages her fingertips, but also a barrier to close out the offenders. A man in a similar situation will wring his hands; the effect is a masculine let's-get-down-to-business gesture while adapting and barriering. A man rubbing his legs is an inborn male approach to counteracting stress. As he rubs his thighs, the contact with his skin releases hormones to comfort him, while at the same time, the aggressive rubbing releases energy. This adaptor is not just for a baseball player on deck. You will also see it in the board room.

Women have a version of the batter-on-deck, too. We've sat in rooms with women who are suddenly "cold" as the meeting heats up. They cross their arms and pet themselves on the elbows and forearms. A learned behavior, it may have started in response to cold, but it has become a strategy for self-comforting and barriering. Because people actually do a variation of the move when they're cold, this tends not to draw attention to discomfort.

The energy transfer affected by adaptors varies greatly from individual to individual and culture to culture. The variations are too numerous to list—this book would turn into a body-language encyclopedia. The one constant is that, typically, men are more tactile than women, which means men's adaptors are easier to identify than women's.

Barriers

A barrier shields the self from threats, whether real or perceived, and demonstrates the need for control. Closing your eyelids, changing your angle of approach, and other subtle moves belong in the mix of those you know well: using hands or arms, desks, counters, books, and computers to put something between your torso and another person. Your choices of objects to use are often subconscious. In proper male fashion, most personal non-object barriering is bigger for men than women. Remember how men think: A little is good, so more is better.

Most often, men move the barrier further away from the body. As a result, the barriers are more evident. These barriers will likely find themselves closer to the person's center of gravity as well. The exception to this is the fig leaf described in Chapter 3. Women have a version of the fig leaf, as well, which is crossing arms in from of the abdomen; it is protection of the primary sex organs (ovaries) in the same way a man protects testes.

Some barriers are meant to be impenetrable. Religious articles that represent faith cannot be safely tampered with; as such, they create the breastplate of God. Some of these barriers are meant for outward observation and others for internal reference only (for example, the Catholic scapula and Mormon temple garments). These barriers do not only protect the wearer, they also tie the wearer to a commitment that takes priority over all else. You cannot overestimate the power of such an object. Although outward representations are more acceptable on women in American culture, can you imagine arguing with a minister who is holding a copy of the Bible as he critiques your immoral behavior? This specific class of men uses the object barrier more effectively than any other in American society. Most men have a tendency to rely on natural barriers.

If men use natural barriers more demonstratively, women use apparel and object barriers more openly. Take the woman who wears a 3-inch long cross. Is this primarily a symbol of religion or mostly a fashion statement? Put the same cross on a middle-aged man. What is the effect? If he's not on the altar in a church, he either looks like a wannabe rock star or a weirdo.

Illustrators

Whereas men may brow-beat, women will be more likely to make their points with the entire body. Head-bobbing and finger-wagging are likely part of the picture. Because men have less of a tendency to engage the entire body and are less likely to gesture wildly, it is no surprise your third-grade teacher could get her point across without shouting. The illustrators used by men are typically uni-channel, such as hands, brow, or perhaps arms.

Even with the tremendous influence of hormones on the system, one cannot over-emphasize the impact of nurture and all of the subprograms added to the human mind throughout the years a human is alive. Simply look at people who have experienced gender reassignment surgery as proof that hormones cannot be the end of the story. Along with human behavior comes a concept of self. Gender identity can be strongly rooted or simply on the surface. Watch the expression of anger in a person who identifies with a gender other than his or her birth gender.

Culture

Because men and women in the same culture confuse the body language of the opposite gender, imagine how easy this becomes across cultures. Culture is like a ghost in the machine. Most cultural influences are so subtle we cannot recognize them. The long-term influence of being exposed to a culture alters our minds and behaviors forever.

Adaptors

Adaptors are the most natural, non-contrived body language that humans possess, primarily because adaptors are not intended to emphasize the verbal. They are for the individual's use only and most do not even realize they are using an adaptor.

Adaptors may be relatively consistent across cultures, but we can quickly make wrong assumptions if we look for something familiar. Just like cognates in a foreign language, for instance, *bizarro* means "gallant" in English, not "bizarre"—assumptions about the meaning of a gesture by someone from another culture will likely trap you in a misunderstanding. If there are so many forms of adaptors that we cannot list them here, imagine what can happen when viewed from outside a culture. Every culture will develop specific taboos and meanings whose origins have long since past from memory. People in these cultures learn that the specific action is taboo by social norming.

Assume you develop an adaptor that is to rub all of your extended fingers and thumb on one hand together while turned upright. This looks somewhat similar to a gesture for money in the United States. Now, let's say your adaptor becomes one that places your other index finger in the cradle created by these extended fingertips. You do it frequently when you're under stress. Now put an Iraqi in the room with you and raise the stress level. His shock and anger would interrupt the meeting because he construes your gesture as a foul insult that questions his parentage.

And as we grow more multi-cultural in our business dealings and social interactions, we'll also have to watch out for the "okay" sign and "thumbs up." Whereas people in the United States would see an "okay" sign, in Greece, Spain, Brazil, and Turkey it is not considered an appropriate gesture. It's either offensive, or it's sexual in nature. And in some Arab nations, the "thumbs up" is a rude sexual gesture.

If the impact of cultural taboos can limit your options on adaptors—truly involuntary gestures—imagine the impact on the more intentional gestures of barriering and illustrating. Male culture alone impacts how American men illustrate their thoughts and barrier themselves. When was the last time you saw an American man purse his lips, hand on hips, flounce, tilt his head, and sigh to make the point of exasperation? That's Nathan Lane in *The Bird Cage*, not Hugh Jackman in *X-Men*. Although any of pieces of body language alone may be acceptable, culture has taught most males that this is simply not acceptable male signaling. When we see this, it signals a different kind of male to the American eye. Male children whose primary caregiver is female may experiment with this signaling but quickly adapt out of it as their role models become male.

Barriers

Americans have a different sensibility about space and hygiene than most other cultures. Americans perceive an intrusion into personal space distressing, and that means any uninvited person needs to stand back to at least arm's length. When viewing the body language of others, Americans may read more into a relationship than is there simply by inference due to proximity. In the Arab world, however, men may stand close enough for noses to touch. There is a famous news photo of an older Palestinian gentleman and an Israeli soldier within fractions of an inch of each other. The soldier is shouting and giving the international signal for "get the hell out of here." At first glance, violence looks imminent until you see the older man has his hand touching the soldier—a sign they are beyond violence. The culture dictates that both men save face and it is exactly what is happening.

Taboos are so strong that we can project an image on to someone based on our own interpretation of their body language. We even anthropomorphize animals to give their body language human meaning. How many times have you heard about a smiling dog? Our own definitions of what body language means transfers to other people and cultures as well.

The Colors of Culture

Even color is cultural and you need to consider it in reading body language. White means innocence and purity in North American culture, but not many others. In Asia, white is the symbol of death. Black means authority in many cultures, but not all. Would Darth Vader be intimidating in fuchsia? How about lime green?

Color has come to connote specific messages in cultures through the ages. Sumptuary law was common, that is, law attempting to regulate consumption of certain resources, and among the behaviors it controlled was the use of selected colors, as well as wearing certain decorated styles of clothing associated with members of the royal family.

The contrast with the practices of modern America is startling—if you were a medieval lord, you would wander the streets of Detroit in shock over the colors used in clothing. We live in a world where an average American can buy clothing in any color he or she wants. We have evolved to a perception that anyone, literally, can dress like royalty. We evolve culturally as a result of that awareness and consumer power. An important characteristic of our society is that we can form tribes on an *ad hoc* basis because we have the resources, creativity, and for the most part, societal acceptance of clothing, accessories, cars, and even buildings with "new" colors: serenity, envy, and daisy.

During the 1970s, if you were "in" as a suburban homeowner you crammed your new split-level with appliances in harvest gold and avocado. You were not "in" if they were still there 10 years later, though. Members of every sub-culture, such as the suburban homeowner, have their own symbols of belonging. Golfers have a look, or a range of colorful looks, that they can enjoy on the golf course and nowhere else. Horseback riders have their own look. Each sub-culture will, through approval and sanction, create its own color and style code.

These sanctions and approvals can take many forms. Approvals come through the use of compliments, adoration, and sanctions, through means ranging from avoidance and unvoiced disapproval all the way to both formal and informal methods of humiliation.

American views of use of color are highly dependent on marketing. If you have set ideas regarding who wears what color, that can impact your view of what the color represents. It's not only the style of the clothing, but also the color of a person's clothing that can cause you to put the person into a category that might not fit. Open your eyes to the message and not the way the color makes you feel.

The Role of Humiliation

Public humiliation as punishment and mockery as a tool of intimidation are just two types of cultural practices that alter a person's body language with the specific intent of affecting his emotional state.

Whether intentionally inflicted or not, humiliation has an effect on the person's body language if endured often enough. Interestingly, it is impossible to predict what this effect will be. If you were teased as a child because you're a redhead, you may give a wink and a nod to another redhead as if there were some great redhead cult that needed to rise up in solidarity. These are people who have taken a bit of ribbing as kids and never outgrown it. Their humiliation is, at this point, self-inflicted. A person who is humiliated continuously either allows the humiliation to become defining, as in the case of the persecuted redhead, or learns to adapt and is no longer humiliated when ridiculed.

From the informal group all the way to highly formalized religious and national organizations, every culture engages in humiliation. Whether openly or subtly, groups rely on compliance to norms to help identify those who are undesirable. This creates a more homogenous society. We need ways to differentiate our monkeys from the other monkeys. If you think this has subsided in the modern Western world, look again. It is still happening, just not at the universal level. Now it's more personalized in smaller groups as society becomes fractionalized.

For the informal approach, watch kids in a school yard practice humiliation. The crueler kids—the bullies—perfect it as an art form until someone trumps them. This humiliation is part of the culture of the second grade (although a frightening number of middle-aged people act as though they're 7 years old). If you do not have the latest shoes, the right haircut, or proper social skills you are chastised—childhood sumptuary law. There are a few reasons for this: first to create a more cohesive culture; second to establish a pecking order; and third, to learn and polish skills that will be used in adult life. Most adults are more subtle and polished, but every adult culture still has some second-grade rules floating around.

In a more formal act of humiliation, Saudis cut off the right hand of convicted thieves, not to stop them from stealing again, but to humiliate them. Their dining practice is to eat from a common plate, and only to take food with the right hand because Arabs use the left hand (often without benefit of toilet paper) to take care of business in the bathroom. Cutting off the right hand of a man cripples him socially.

What happens to the repeat offender, you might ask? Starvation? No, his fellow citizens will simply remove his left foot. With his left hand he can operate a crutch, but not attend too many social engagements. Needless to say, Saudi Arabia has a much lower rate of stealing than the United States.

Sanctions related to humiliating body language can take many forms. They come from avoidance and unvoiced disapproval all the way through blatant humiliation, both formal and informal.

Not all signaling from the humiliated will be the beaten-down kind. Self-loathing induced by constant humiliation can lead to outward displays of narcissism. Look for the impact and the body language of submission in group dynamics.

Pop Culture Prejudice

In the 2006–2007 *Survivor* episodes filmed on the Cook Islands, the long-running reality TV show featured tribes segregated by race. At first, this jolted and offended lots of fans and foes of the series. As the idea got second consideration from many people, however, the pink elephant in the room became visible: Humans do tend to go toward their own. If "your own" is visibly defined by features and color, then it's easy to find your brethren. In other words, in the thinking of the show's producers, if five African-Americans, five Asians, five Caucasians, and five Hispanics find themselves stranded on an island without the benefit of television cameras, there is a high likelihood that they will hang out with people of their own race *if* they have nothing more binding than race. Race can easily become secondary, however, to nationalism, or fraternal bonding such as common organizations or religious affiliation. It's an exercise predicated on the operation of tribal distinctions at their most basic level: "You don't look like me" or "You do look like me."

Look at your own association preference—no judgment and no need to disclose it to anyone else—as you are trying to read others. It can be one of the most blinding filters.

Projection

In the beginning of this book we asked you to suspend the very thing that makes you human: your overdeveloped mind. Now we are at the crux of the matter. Most of the things we already covered in this chapter create templates for you to project on to someone. All of that programming given to you by your parents, school, religion, media, government, and personal relationships can cloud your vision to what you are seeing.

Projection means you see what you want to see.

Let's start with the elderly and disabled. We project weakness of all kinds on to a person who has any weakness of body. We refuse to believe that a frail-looking senior citizen can murder or that someone in a wheelchair could commit a terrorist act. And when we accuse someone like that of a crime, what are we upright, healthy folks likely to feel? Guilt. That's a big mistake—normal, but it's the same reason why a woman such as serial killer Aileen Wuornos could get away with murder. She was a woman, after all. How dangerous could she be?

When we look at someone who is elderly or disabled, even someone who is young and sick, or "the weaker sex," some strong emotions may run beneath our responses and affect them. We see our humanity, our fragility, our vulnerability.

Part of it may be that that other person doesn't have the repertoire of body language that makes us feel comfortable. Subconsciously, we conclude that our own communication is curtailed by her physical limitations.

In writing this book, we did some people watching on a street in a tourist town, in stores, at a coffee shop, and in bars. We were visiting with one of Maryann's friends whose hometown bar scene could be characterized by the word "tame," but she thought one of them might have a little more action than the others. Never having been there, we wondered how she arrived at that conclusion. Rumors. Hearsay. A trip to one of the bars helped illuminate the effects of projection, especially how it interferes with a real understanding of body language.

Maryann's friend took one look at the waitress and thought she had her pegged. She read the tattoo, suggestive top, and sexy walk as signs of a certain kind of person. A very different person came over to meet us, however. The tattoo was of her childrens' names interlaced around her arm. Up close, the top looked more like a good choice for a hot summer day than part of a come-hither wardrobe. And I would not have called her walk sexy; that's a descriptor coming from someone who projected that an attractive woman with a tattoo and halter top would have a sexy walk. An accurate interpretation of the woman's body language would use words such as *open*, *vulnerable*, and *attentive*.

What is the ape in this photo doing?

a. He's sucking his thumb to reduce stress.

b. He's trying to tell you he has a toothache.

c. He has his thumb in his mouth.

Eliminate any projection or conjecture from your evaluation and the only answer that's valid is (c).

Exercise

Do something similar to what we did: Walk into an environment where you would not normally go. Depending on who you are, that could be a library, a bowling alley, a church, or a gym. Allow your projections to take hold as you observe people. Make a point of striking up a conversation with at least one of the people you have "pegged." Did you have any surprises and, if so, what did they tell you about yourself?

By nature, people filter everything we see and hear. This well-developed adult brain is constantly trying to put things in context, to create schemas that work in our world, to find patterns and connections. You must subdue that drive to be good at reading body language. You need to stop forcing things to make sense and to focus solely on what people do and the similarities and differences between what they do.

Our lives are filled with rituals and routines that have made us successful or not. These strongly held beliefs and strategies color everything we see, hear, and do. Some of us have created elaborate tactics that prey on the rituals others have in place and we'll explore some very public examples of this in Part III. Trying to overlay all new information onto an old grid taints the information. Your filters will prevent you from seeing clearly. Suspend or at least quantify the impact these filters are having on what you see before you try to analyze what you are seeing.

Caricatures and stereotypes overemphasize at least one trait that people can identify easily about a person or group. These super-typical mannerisms and cultural differences still exist, but outside of some comedy clubs, it's no longer acceptable to use them to characterize a group. In an effort to honor diverse traditions and not hurt anyone's feelings—the long way of saying "be politically correct"—we have shoved most of these down society's linguistic garbage disposal. Ah! But out of sight does not mean out of mind. Though some of these have faded from public view, they still inhabit our conscious and subconscious. The result is a powerful filter that can blind the mind's eye.

Projection is the most dangerous blinder you can put on, and its real power derives from other things we talked about in this chapter—prejudices rooted in culture and gender. You have to ask yourself the question "Which group of people am I biased against?" You may be prejudiced against 5-foot blondes who went to Catholic school and have perfect grammar. Not a bad group to most of us, but if you don't like them, you must identify your prejudice and look carefully at that group's body language if you want to communicate with them.

Other things can blind our vision as well, such as reading a book by an expert and taking everything at face value without adapting it to fit your own mind, personality, and the situation. This R.E.A.D. system means that you need to learn to look at a person and decide what something means when that particular person does it, and in a particular context. No book can do that. Relying on a laundry list of gestures and drawing conclusions, such as "hands on hips means…" is the worst kind of projection.

By now you should see that you are developing your own kind of body language lexicon—one that is different from anyone else's. This is because you have experiences that have influenced your view. Hold on to those experiences; they will be very useful in the "decide" phase.

What's likely to really trip you up, though? Think back to the walking-while-thinking-of-a-bad-day exercise. The emotional down shifted your posture and balance to low gear. Simply being in an emotional slump can profoundly skew your perception of another person's body language. You need to get past that down state, past your high state, past your own mood if you want to be really skilled at reading body language.

7

Making It Personal

In the process of review, you taught *yourself* the second piece: evaluate, that is, look for the meaning of actions. You built on the knowledge of movements with an understanding of moods and other factors that influence body language like meta-behaviors, primarily mirroring, and rituals. You have also seen how your preconceived notions can filter what you are seeing, or even blind you.

Undoubtedly, you have begun to place people on bell curves to organize your perceptions. This is human nature, but it is difficult to research the chimps when you are one of them. You need a couple of other tools to help you understand exactly what this all means, namely, the individual's norm and context. These tools will help you to complete the final step of the interpretive process: the "A" we began covering in the last chapter. Once you have "A," analyzed, what the pieces and parts mean when you put them together, you can "D," decide, how you will use that knowledge.

Yes, we know you do this instinctively already and we do not want you to lose that. What we want you to do is train your brain to operate methodically in the "R" and "E" phases to allow you to analyze what you are seeing. It's a cognitive, not an emotional, exercise. If you are already intuitive and afraid you will mess that up, don't worry. You will use both skills moving forward: intuition, or gut, with a good tool set to validate.

This analysis is now going to ask you to put the thinking person and the adult back in charge. You don't need the childlike data collection. Now you need to start to use that education, experience, street smarts, male or female brain, and intellectual capacity to pare down all of this into something meaningful. We are going to give you some additional things to think about as you analyze what you have observed—but *your* knowledge is important now.

An Individual's Norm

When Data, the android on *Star Trek: The Next Generation*, has determined his chips have a glitch, he states that he is "not functioning within normal parameters." That's normal parameters *for him*. Even the quirkiest of personalities has a "normal" for him.

You can even determine an individual's normal patterns if he is affected by illness or genetic aberration if you baseline. For example, Greg has a good friend who has Tourette's syndrome, a type of disorder involving involuntary, repetitive movements and vocalizations. These involuntary actions are part of *his* normal.

You can read the emotions and intentions of someone like this as well as you can read someone unaffected by such a disorder by taking two steps:

1. Turning off the filters related to normal/abnormal that would blind you.
2. Pay attention to what is normal for him.

This is baselining. Baselining is a much simpler exercise with most people, although even people without movement disorders can have strange idiosyncrasies. By now, you likely have seen a few for yourself, such as strange grooming behaviors, self-petting, or odd food rituals. You may have even noticed a couple of your own, because we all have them.

We started this book by defining communication and breaking it into vocal, verbal, and non-verbal categories. Let's use this model for analyzing what is normal for an individual.

Verbal: Servant of the Will

By "will" we mean the conscious mind, the forefront of being human. Though "verbal" may be the servant of the will, occasionally the *sub*conscious of a person will let you look into his mind through word use as well. Every person has a style of word usage that is normal for that individual. Our choice of words is tempered by education, culture, self-image, and how we want to be perceived.

When someone's word pattern changes, you can usually track that change to a reason. If you are talking to someone who normally has a pattern of plain, simple English, for instance, and she shifts to an elaborate soliloquy about a product, what does that tell you? She read or heard some propaganda and committed a few phrases to memory. Your ears immediately alert you to a deviation from that person's verbal baseline. The words are too fancy or studied, or perhaps too descriptive about a subject that it's unlikely the person is well-versed in it. The words don't fit the person, the moment, or the emotion the person seems to want to convey. Maryann went to a wine tasting recently and the young woman offering the tasting was new to the job and got her stock phrases a little mixed up. Suddenly a "hint of vanilla," and "rather unctuous" got stuck in all the wrong places. There were some fairly odd suggestions on food pairings as well. A lot more wines apparently go with Gruyere cheese than anyone ever suspected.

Similarly, the shift to simpler language can represent what is going on in a person's head. Perhaps she is dumbing down to play you—an old trick of some not-so-dumb blondes. Or is he trying to sound less intelligent to make you feel comfortable? Although he's not the first President of the United States to do this, Barack Obama would tactically drop "ing" from the end of some of his words, ostensibly to sound more like the people he was addressing. You can also watch for length of sentence and pronoun choice to better understand a person's intentions, distractions, and so on. Pronoun shift from "I" to "we" can mean he wants to share the blame for something, for example, as in "We have to go now" early into a party that only he finds boring. The list is extensive, but a baseline is easy to develop. Just let your brain notice when something is unusual and then ask why.

Vocal: Servant of the Highest Bidder

Vocal is the "servant of the highest bidder" because, under enough stress, the voice will sell out the will and tell you exactly what the mind contains. Volumes could be written about different tones and their meaning; everyone reading this book has heard these utterances. Remember your mother or some teacher wagging a finger at you saying, "It's not what you said, it's the way you said it!" If the human voice was the first musical instrument, it was also likely the first instrument of torture. Even a pre-human ancestor without a spoken verbal language probably got this point across with a shriek or grunt.

Stress causes a rise in vocal pitch. A stressed person will have clipped tones and a strained sound to the voice. Add a bit of heavy emotion—sorrow, anger, joy, uncertainty—and the vocal chords themselves respond similar to the strings of a musical instrument. Without any choice, the vocal has sold out to the highest bidder, leaving the will to fend for itself with simple words.

Try this with your dog, cat, horse, or any other animal that responds to your voice: Tell her how much you love her in a gruff, angry tone of voice.

How did she respond? Now tell her you are dumping her at the pound and use a happy baby-talk voice. How did she respond? People respond similarly. You sound loving, so you can't possibly want to beat me up.

The best way to find out a person's baseline for normal vocal utterances is to observe him or her for a short period of time in a non-stressful environment. How does your boss sound when he is secretive, maybe doing nothing more than telling his wife he loves her at the end of a phone conversation? His tone changes as he fears how the simple statement will be perceived by his subordinates. How does he demonstrate he has lost his patience even when masking?

Non-Verbal: Servant to the Mind

Gesturing, typically under the control of the will, can occasionally break out of the cage. This is primarily because gesturing is a learned trait, as is verbal, and as such, is subject to rules about common usage and taboos, just as the verbal is.

Gestures represent entire thoughts, so they serve as the clearest example of the correlation between verbal and non-verbal. They mean something specific in a particular culture and you can also express that specific idea in words. Quite understandably, then, this class of non-verbal is subjected to the same rules of control and outburst as the verbal. Occasionally, a gesture may resemble something you know, so you assume it has the same meaning, just as you might assume that a false cognate like bizarro means "bizarre" instead of gallant.

All other non-verbal communication serves the mind, however, with little regard for the will. While the will of the young manager says, "Yes, sir!" to the boss, his mind places him above that kind of subservient response. The young man's hands give him away as he places them on his hips and wrinkles his brow.

You want to look at the holistic view of an individual's body language while you notice the bits and pieces. If he projects an angry mood overall, but you see a playfulness about the eyes, what is the message?

If I were to see this in a very intelligent man I would take it as a danger signal. The same signal coming from a middle-aged woman can mean something entirely different. Same picture, but different brushstrokes on the canvas. The only way you can be sure is by baselining the individual. For example, you may know a woman whose normal pattern relies on a ritualistic harshness when she's angry, but in a particular instance, you see a playfulness in her eye and a softening of her features. You conclude you may have a chance to win this one; it is all in how you play it.

Now go back to the man with the same expression and compare and contrast the brushstrokes.

- Does the person's body language holistically support the message he is trying to send?
- Will his message differ when he's with the guys and with his mate?
- Is his behavior similar to others of his kind? In other words, what is the norm not only for his culture, but also for males within his culture?

You have decided he is not exactly super-typical, but he does distinguish himself with certain gestures and postures. You have observed scalp to soles and mentally recorded data about clothing and other indicators of status. Next, you must discover what body language is unique to him.

By its nature, this exercise is about rebuilding some of those stereotypes, but with meaning about how the group this animal comes from behaves. That allows you a cultural baseline instead of one of your own invention. Within a colony of chimps, however, there is diversity and that is what drives the next step: Baseline a micro component of the colony—the individual.

Baselining Mechanics

You need to ask questions that you know the answer to—a stage in your baselining activity whether you are hunting for verbal clues or behavioral clues. These should be simple questions that get his opinion about the best beer, or where to find a bicycle tire. Regardless of what the questions address, your aim is finding his norm, so you have to be non-confrontational at first. Remember your cataloging exercises because they come into play here. Analyze what is normal.

- What is his normal way of looking around?
- How does he stand/sit when relaxed?
- At what level does he normally gesture—waist-high or a little above the waist? How would you describe his gestures when relaxed? Open, energetic, and so on?

- Where do his eyes access as he recalls data? (The test for memory versus construct is in Chapter 3.)

- How does he respond when you ask about his opinion on a nonthreatening topic, such as the best restaurant in town?

The responses give you insights, such as the following: After you have collected this baseline information, you ask him why Judy in sales flew to Vancouver last week instead of doing her usual site visit to San Diego. If he responds with facts, but his body language says "opinion," with things like a request for approval, then red flags should go up.

Use the holistic approach to create a picture of what is normal for the particular person. This is not a month-long study of the monkey. This is a quick review of the person followed by an evaluation to note what stands out about this particular person.

We are all products of our environment, with culture playing an insidious role in who we become. We get away with something, and it becomes a habit. We develop strategies for survival, and they work, so we repeat them. Describe your habits and strategies. When you feel threatened, do you demonstrate your strength by becoming bigger, or do you shrink so that the threat will underestimate you until you can pounce? The most successful among us have created many-layered approaches to communication and may broadcast strength and vulnerability at the same time to different audiences.

Baselining Do's and Don'ts

Do: Ask questions that require a narrative response.

Do Not: Ask yes-or-no questions.

A premise of baselining for eye movement is that the person must be forced to access certain portions of his brain, such as the visual and auditory centers. A yes-or-no question probably will not get the job done. For example, if your aim is to see whether his eyes move left or right to access memory, you would not ask, "Do you live on that street where lightning struck a tree last year?" You would say, "I think I know the neighborhood where you live. What are some of the landmarks around there?"

Do: Sense and intuit.

Do Not: Assume and project.

Your eyes and ears will collect a great deal of information, but what if those senses pick up "honesty," but you still feel something's wrong? Pathological liars, con men, and interrogators such as Greg have either natural or cultivated skills of deception. With interrogators, you need to rely on intuition, too. When they become a glossy copy of self, you know something isn't right.

Women have an anatomical advantage because they have a larger corpus callosum than a man. This thick collection of nerve fibers that connects the left and right hemispheres of the brain gives women the practical benefit of signals crossing from the left (logical) to the right side (creative) of the brain, and vice versa, very quickly. In effect, women have a revolving door between the hemispheres that enables agile movement back and forth. Men have to open a locked door between them before they move to the other side. Intuition involves both feelings and facts, so you can see how the "female" brain supports it.

Assumptions and projections clog your ability to sense and intuit information about someone. Baselining is focused on one person at a time, and carrying certain assumptions as you go into an experience, or projecting your own behavior and style of communicating on someone, can give you false readings.

Do: Take cultural and regional differences into consideration.

Do Not: Let prejudice, notions, or stereotypes affect baselining.

Refer back to Chapter 2 to raise your awareness of cultural issues and differences. In short, pay attention to the many facets of the person you're baselining, but don't make snap judgments based on your biases.

Do: Baseline deliberately, as needed.

Do Not: Use the techniques habitually.

These are serious skills of an interrogator, not party tricks. You can save yourself time, aggravation, and heartache by using them in the early stages of dating, but if you start practicing on everyone, people will catch on and feel uncomfortable around you.

Context

What do you see in this photo? Is the woman blocking someone out or simply standing proudly? Is that fist-to-hip gesture on the man an arrogant cocky smirk aimed at the photographer for a reason, or is it simply a pose? What about the kid sitting on the hood of the car? And why the distance? Take a minute without reading any further and decide what all of this means. As you read through the chapter, you will find out the true story in the appropriate section.

No amount of reading can teach you to put things in context. If your husband came home covered in blood with his belt missing and told you he used his belt for a tourniquet to save a life—his head hanging down to the right and looking shaken—you would believe him. In contrast, if he came home freshly showered, in the same clothes he had on that morning, but no belt, and tells you the same story with his head hung down to the right and looking shaken, what do you assume?

Imagine the permutations. Now you get to engage your well-developed, adult brain by combining your newfound knowledge with years of human experience. You have reached the "A" in R.E.A.D., with an emphasis on the skill of putting behaviors in context.

Factors Influencing Context

Factors we want to highlight here are where the body language occurs, your subject's companions, and various aspects of timing.

Location

"Location" refers to where you see the body language. Is it in a bar? At church? At work? In the airport? A car? Each will set expectations of how the person should behave. For instance, when driving in a car, do you pick your nose? (Don't lie. We've seen you.) If a man's home is his castle, his car is his portable castle. People feel safe in this very personal space. Body language is natural; you can see exaggerated body language when a person talks on the phone when driving alone. Why? Most of us have brains that function well with only one or two tasks at hand—even the brains of the Millennials and Gen Z that grew up multi-tasking with the aid of handfuls of gadgets. When you go past your task limit, something has to be compromised. It will likely be the high-end polished body language, as we forget someone may be looking.

The Airport

The airport has a pronounced effect because people are so disengaged with others. You walk from terminal to terminal, often without noticing others. The body language is artificial, in part because people are pack animals at the airport. You have the unnatural task of carrying or rolling an additional 50 pounds behind you and hurrying to make a schedule. Think back to the discussion of focus: If you are in the airport for the first time, or one of the first few times, you are still out of place and that shows in your body language. The seasoned traveler (at least the ones who don't thrive on anxiety) arrives with just the right amount of time to get to her destination; moving around the airport seems as comfortable as walking from one office to another. Regardless of the sensibility, the airport is not usually a social engagement.

Church, Work, or Other Formal Setting

Church may be the ultimate in formal settings with its rituals clearly defined. If it is the most formal for fear of retribution from God, at least God forgives; bosses rarely do. If you watch Sunday Mass broadcast on television from a big cathedral, you will be struck by how many people follow the ritual, but look thoroughly indifferent. Can you imagine sitting in front of your boss with this body language? If so, what about the CEO of your company? It is natural for the alpha to make you uncomfortable? At work, the trappings of the alpha are omnipresent. Clandestine routines emerge so you can communicate things you do not want the alpha to see. How do you hide personal Internet use at work? Even when you behave naturally at work, you are displaying your normal work-self, not the person you are with a tribe of old friends or other micro-culture. Your body language will be more formal and less natural. The more iconic the setting, the less natural the body language.

An Unknown Place

When Greg first joined the Army, another 18-year old kid walked into the hotel they were staying in the night before their physicals. As Greg walked onto the elevator, the other teenager followed him with a halting, timid gait. He held his arms quietly by his side. "Everything okay?" Greg asked. He answered, "I am from Buena Vista (pronounced "bewna vista" in that part of the South) and I have never seen an elevator." Your uneasiness bleeds through when you are in totally unfamiliar surroundings and have no frame of reference. Even if you muster the nerve to act cavalierly, your mind is still reaching for more data to create a more familiar picture and your body language will show it.

Companions

Friends, lovers, coworkers, relative strangers—your interaction with them affects how you present yourself, how much stress or raw emotion is present, and to what extend your culture-specific gestures show up.

Opposite Sex (Or Whatever Sex Attracts You)

Place one very attractive young woman in the presence of 10 heterosexual men around her age. What kind of body language will you get from her? Vulnerability and softening to look more appealing and feminine. From the men? Likely an exaggerated strut, hands-on-hips framing genitalia with overly blocky masculine moves. If this behavior yields rewards, what is the long-term impact for the person—either man or woman?

Super-Typical People

When traveling with superiors, whether a boss or simply someone you perceive as super-typical, your body language will be constricted. Think of the expression "big fish in a small pond." The cliché refers to having the ability to be super-typical in a defined and confined environment. When you are the super-typical, your body language is uninhibited and expansive. When you perceive yourself as typical or sub-typical, you may limit how demonstrative you are with body language.

If being in the company of the super-typical causes you anxious moments, what happens when you are in the company of the sub-typical who appears to be super-typical? How can that happen? They know the routines of the culture better than you do.

Every year, Estes Park, Colorado, hosts the largest Scottish Highlands Festival in North America. On the fairgrounds, you'll see hundreds of men in kilts and people of all ages in period costumes spanning a thousand years of Scottish history. It was not the least bit odd to see these people wandering around town in their outfits in the days just prior to the festival. The whole town was getting into the spirit and created a context for these people to broadcast their Scottish heritage.

In short, everyone wanted to belong, and many of the people who knew the traditions and had the right costumes—the people others tried to emulate—included those we'd probably label sub-typical in a different environment.

Antagonists

When a person is in a conflict of any type, the body language will show it. How fluid can your behavior be when your mind is rigidly set against the person you are standing next to? Not all antagonists arouse a sense of conflict, however. Some cause pain such as disappointment, frustration, or resentment.

The photo earlier in the chapter is Greg's father, grandmother, and grandfather on one of his estranged grandfather's visits. He left weeks before Greg's father was born and moved on to various other pastures, remarrying every few years. Envision the conflict and anger that his grandmother felt when he finally showed up again—moments before this photo was taken. Abandoned by him in 1938, she was a devout Christian woman from the Deep South who suddenly had complete responsibility for two sons while pregnant with a third. Her husband went out "to get salt" and came back when Greg's father was a teenager. Now what do the folded arms mean to you? She had worked in the Georgia cotton fields to support her sons; she was physically and emotionally strong and proud. Why is he standing so cocky? Can we write him off as a callous philanderer, a selfish and self-indulgent nomad? This is a man who, at the age of 35, went ashore on D-Day with the 29th Infantry Division. To some extent, that earned him the right to look cocky. Why does the kid look quietly pleased? Well, he's happy that Dad is home.

The body language of conflict would look much different from what we are seeing here. This photo captures resentment. She may stand near him, but he is definitely feeling the cold shoulder. These two people lived on the same street less than a block away for years before his death and never even waved to one another.

Time

This is not just a time-of-day or time-of-year issue, as in Christmas Day or a birthday. Time as a factor in analyzing context relates to the way a gesture fits into a whole sequence of actions. When did the action you are analyzing take place, that is, what gestures preceded it and followed it? How long did it take to complete the gesture?

If you've ever seen a silent movie, in which movements seem faster than normal, you've observed the influence of timing on the meaning of a gesture. An actress portraying grief will put her head down, bring it up to talk and cry, put it down again, and repeat the process. It looks funny instead of sad to us, because the speed makes it look as though the grieving widow is bobbing her head up and down in a "yes" gesture.

Consider the range of possibilities in this example: A young woman smiles at you, but breaks eye contact quickly. Is this enough information to make the decision about approaching her? Does the type of smile have greater significance than the duration of her glance? How important is where her eyes shifted after that? Donald Trump has a habit of turning his face away from the camera while maintaining eye contact until the last second to punctuate a smug thought. Does it endear and create trust? Or does it create uncertainty?

Now consider the range of possibilities created by this kind of eye contact: A young man smiles at you and stares. It is a friendly smile, but without any brow movement, so he doesn't recognize you. He continues the prolonged eye contact for what seems like an eternity, even though it's only 10 seconds. How important is the type of smile in this case? Is your normal reaction fear? Anger? Annoyance? Curiosity? What other factors of timing in his body movement affect your response? If the young man bore multiple tattoos, and was wearing a beat-up hunting jacket, how would you react if he quickly shoved his hand inside his jacket as he stared at you? Now take this same young man, tattoos and all. He gives you a lingering stare with a blank face. The jaw is slack; his eyes are focused somewhere beyond you; his gate is ambling and disconcerted; and his skin, pale. These are signs of shock, and his sense of timing will be way off—so far off that even if he does do some of the same actions as the person I described previously, your reaction would probably be curiosity or sympathy, rather than fear.

Personal Strategy

Humans have an ingenious ability to find what works. Once we discover what works, we use it until it doesn't.

When you were a child, the first strategy you learned was to shake your head to stop something from happening. You used that until you discovered the word no, which you probably repeated until your parents wanted to throw you out of the house. In short, it stopped working for you.

As "no" failed, you learned others strategies to stop things from happening. You never completely discarded the old ones; you simply put them away or incorporated them into your much more polished scheme.

As your age and your intelligence about how the world works matures, your strategy for dealing with the world evolves as well. Because each of us is a unique collection of genes and experiences, this strategy is unique as well. They sometimes create a sort of individual brand that's key to the person's existence.

The real art to reading body language and thus analyzing (the "A" in R.E.A.D.) what something means, is to learn to vivisect these strategies and see the rituals, adaptors, barriers, illustrators, and gesturing for what they really are: a language specific to the person who is using it.

Your experiences and knowledge will give you a unique ability to do this. You have the skill to see the minutia as a child would, a model for the holistic, and the understanding of context won from years of living. Now you need to use those tools to look at the communication strategy of your subject. How much of what he is saying with his body is intentional? How much is involuntary? Are the two aligned? Which is the most reliable?

In the next chapter, we will focus your attention on communication strategies of people in the limelight to see what works for them...at least most of the time.

Part III:
Applying the Skill

8

Politicians, Pundits, and Stars

Every time a person is rewarded for a behavior, the behavior becomes entrenched. The toddler shakes her head "no." It works. She does it again and again. Adults are those children covered in more layers of life. When something works, you keep it in your repertoire and build on it.

When you hit conflict or simply need to influence someone, you revert to a successful model. Some of these behaviors will be conscious and intentional, and others will be adaptors that have worked for so long they become second nature. The following list contains a few strategy models. Look around you and create your own list based on what you observe, so that it becomes a tool for you to use in the "D" of R.E.A.D.

- The Holy Warrior
- I'm Just a Girl
- The Flirt
- There is Nothing to See Here
- The Blamer
- Bubble Boy/Bubble Girl
- The Magician
- The Ringmaster
- The Car Salesman

The intentional or unintentional behavior a person relies on for conflict and influence has a downside that gives you clues to what is really going on in his head: The model is not all-encompassing. The supporting body language is often missing. You can detect irregularities. When the model does not work, the person may flounder in attempts to be convincing.

The Holy Warrior creates an image that is beyond reproach by bonding to a Cause. Simply being associated with the Cause assuages his guilt in other areas. If you manage to attack his behavior, he will quickly become indignant—chin up, enunciating more clearly—so that you understand his point of view because, obviously, you must have missed it the first time. He stays on topic, which is the Cause, and off of topics or discussions that raise questions about whether or not he has the knowledge and skills to say what he's saying. This is commonly used by the moral hijackers among the super-typical, who understand little about the whole issue, but lift themselves to the role of saint for the Cause.

I'm Just a Girl is most often used by women in a male-dominated industry. Younger women might also use it successfully against someone who is matronly and self-consumed. The woman can play up the most feminine of her characteristics and emotional (weak) body language to look vulnerable and more feminine. This body language plays on the innate ability to make men more protective and less fierce. She plays up the "I'm just a girl" to get men to either cease attack or influence behavior in some way. Many women have perfected this in personal relationships as well by quietly allowing the men in their lives to believe they are in control.

The Flirt may rely on a variety of behaviors, and not necessarily sexual ones. In our dictionary, flirting means making emotional contact with someone, and filling the air with energy. It can be done between the same sex or opposite sexes. You know you've encountered a flirt when, regardless of how far you are from him physically, he seems close. There is no dead air between the two you. A skilled flirt can connect with dozens or even thousands of people at the same time, with each one certain that the connection is personal. Some politicians do it through speech and some musicians do it through song. A big reason why movie and TV viewers can feel attached to stars is the artificial closeness that the camera creates. The flirt takes your mind off of everything except the interchange. You suspend looking at body language and may not even notice content.

Whether you're a litigator, an interrogator, or a public relations professional, flirting is a requisite skill. We think almost anyone can learn enough to be an expert on any subject in two hours or less, and we've even written a book about that, too. All you need is an understanding of where the issue intersects the person—a skill inherent in flirting. If you can understand what about another person's profession keeps him up at night, you and he have an emotional connection. You will overlook hygiene, dress, and mannerisms in someone with whom you can identify. After all, when you have that connection, anything negative about that person reflects on you.

There Is Nothing to See Here can have several variations, the simplest of which is self-deprecation to the point that others underestimate the person. This is the 50-year-old barista at your local Starbucks who retired 14 years ago when his technology start-up was acquired by a giant Silicon Valley company. He's the relaxed, friendly guy everyone assumes has no ambition and happens to be worth $24 million. This is a play on a stereotype—remember that filter? Once customers write him off as just a happy-go-lucky guy, he can get them to talk about kinds of things and they don't feel threatened by him in the least. Meanwhile, he's putting them all into his brilliant debut novel. People rarely change their first impressions.

I'm Just a Kid involves tactics similar to playing on femininity. A young person can play naïve and uninformed easily with a self-consumed person who is older. This is the simplest for young people to pull off because their body language is likely less polished and fits the profile. Consider how it could work in an office, though, with a middle-aged worker shrugging her shoulders and looking a little lost after making a mistake. She looks up at her supervisor as if to say, "You are so much wiser and more competent than I am. I feel like I'm just a kid compared to you."

The Blamer preys on the fact that no one likes to be accused. Human nature drives you to deny or defend, which focuses all energy internally looking for that fact or plea that will change others' minds. This ploy successfully blinds the eye of an opponent; it is one strategy that is difficult to fight. You need to pause and watch the accuser's body language to know whether it is a ploy or an actual attack the person thinks has merit. The next time you watch Kanye West interact with other people, think of this category of behavior.

The Bubble Boy/Bubble Girl observes other people carefully, but pulls back from intimate contact—especially in public. They have strategies to keep themselves separate, whether through the use of barriers or by simply leaving the room. When out with the guys, Bubble Boy might cheer for the home team, but he won't do it with the raucous fist-pumping enthusiasm of the others. Bubble Girl may enjoy hanging with her friends, but instead of cooing and ooing over a great pair of shoes, she'll say, "They're nice!" She stays actively involved with what matters, but just out of reach of the consequence.

The Magician has overlap with other strategies, which are basically variations with the same objective: If I can take your eyes off my body language for a moment, maybe you will miss the facts. Nevertheless, we separate out

The Magician because there is an entire class of people who use movement of hands, feet, and objects to mask body language entirely. Examples are the guy who moves in very close and whispers to make you feel uncomfortable. The distraction makes you miss the rest of his body language. Or the woman who unfastens a few buttons so you can peek at her surgeon's handiwork. These outrageous moves will accomplish the goal of taking your mind off something else. A person may even use some other prop such as an Apple watch. All of them use your tendency to keep your eye on the ball to effect the desired result.

The Car Salesman subscribes to the adage, "If you can't dazzle them with brilliance, baffle them with bullshit." Everyone has met the guy who sounds as though he has swallowed the *Guinness Book of World Records*. When his strategy works, he carries off the same sleight-of-hand tricks as The Magician. It falls apart when you challenge his understanding of the facts he quotes. He takes you off a sensitive topic that would make him look bad by tossing out, "Every minute we do nothing in Vulgaria, three children die." He becomes adept at tying anything back to some obscure fact that is difficult to verify and only tangentially germane to the topic. The reason a person akin to this survives is that most people are intimidated by his "knowledge" and the rest follow another well-known adage, "Never argue with an idiot; he will beat you down to his level and win with experience."

The Ringmaster enters the room with a deliberate, commanding presence. It may be quiet and focused or grandiose and loud. The Ringmaster owns the space. Donald Trump taking center stage to introduce his wife's speech at the 2016 Republican National Convention represents the image perfectly: Backlit and appearing to walk on air because of a smoke machine, he walked with an ambling gate to the podium to the tune of Queen's "We Are The Champions." Non-billionaire Ringmasters don't enter a room with a smoke machine, but they can still make you believe that they are elevated above the masses by the sheer force of their will and power. The Ringmaster is the center of attention at all times, unless he chooses not to be. If you try to step up and take the lead, you are "put in your place" by a canned tactic. Trump very effectively demonstrated the use of this by tagging his opponents in the primary debates with titles like Lying Ted and Little Marco with the timing of a circus ringmaster. The more opponents, the more targets. What a Ringmaster says and does directs the flow the conversation and energy in the room. Regardless of what other people have to say, it's only his opinion that really matters.

The permutations are varied. The thing they all have in common is a ploy to distract your mind from the obvious things a toddler would see, and to bring you around to his way of thinking. Build your own list. Here's one to start with: **The Whisperer** is a person who manipulates through gentle....

Put your new categories to work by examining strategies of the rich and famous, and noticing when they fail as well as when they succeed. Elections, news, and red-carpet events will now have a new dimension for you. Instead of wondering why you feel distrust or disgust about a politician, you have the eye to spot verbal and non-verbal warning signs. And are the stars you love to love and love to hate really deserving of all that emotion?

As we take you through studies of public figures, watch some video clips of the people and situations referenced here. See if you come to the same conclusions we did and, if you don't, consider how projection, gender (yours and the other person's), ideology, and other elements may have influenced your thinking.

The Clintons

Love them or hate them, both Bill and Hillary have had a major presence in U.S. politics and international affairs for more than two decades. Both have developed strategies—some more successful than others—for putting off prying eyes. They are two very different personalities who have adapted to the micro-culture of their personal relationship, and used contrasting personal styles to elicit essentially the same results from fellow politicians, as well as millions of Americans.

In looking through her book *Living History* (Simon & Schuster, 2003), we see "old Bill" and "old Hillary"—not literally, of course, but an earlier incarnation of both people than those we know today. They are still a couple with contrasting body-language styles, but they would not be described the same way now. Bill was the life of the party, and Hillary, the grounded one. His focus was broad, often leaning toward her while maintaining the attention of the cameras. Her focus was narrow, that is, toward the cameras. That suggests one primarily thing they have in common: They both have a burning need for approval and the influence that comes with it.

Bill Clinton

Bill Clinton is an example of someone who used to define the Flirt category. He was the Flirt in Chief. When he was President of the United States, his charm was robust and he communicated with tremendous power. He perfected the use of his whole hand and arm—not just arm and one finger—in punctuating a point. In the decades since he was in office, however, the vitality has drained out of his body. He still shows signs of the Flirt, but his body language lacks the allure it used to have. Did Bill Clinton somehow lose his magic touch? Not exactly. He got older. He went through normal changes that included health issues, weight change, wrinkles, and sagging skin—all of which affect the way a person's vocal and movement patterns change.

He's still the Flirt in that people who barely know him might say, "It was like talking to someone you have known all your life, and he was focused on only me while we spoke." He is generally not distracted openly and intently focuses on whomever he is speaking to. He fills the air and takes distance away, in part through eye contact, but in equal part through inviting illustrators and regulators. This is the same kind of "flirt" a toddler does: singularity of purpose in focusing on the individual, and capturing a temporary space.

Hillary Clinton

Hillary Clinton needs to be covered almost as two different people because her baseline has changed since she began her run for the White House in the 2016 election cycle. When we analyzed her body language in a previous book, we categorized her as a Holy Warrior. She still is, but she has better signaling than previously, so we'll refer to her as Hillary 1 and Hillary 2.

To describe Hillary 1's style as anything more than wooden or mechanical, you would need to see her "on cause." She was tethered to the text, whether her statement was a few sentences or a few pages. Whether she was actually reading is a central question, but it appeared as though she were barriering herself rather than needing the words on the page. Her habit of "reading" invited criticism, including a jab from former Secretary of Defense Donald Rumsfeld. In a Senate probe in response to the Secretary, then-Senator Clinton once again read her brief comment from a prepared statement and the Secretary took shots at her because of it. She held her lips pursed, and had the tone of voice of a prim grammar-school teacher as she chided the Secretary for his and President Bush's failures. Hillary 1 was at her best when on cause in that manner. How can you respond to her attacks? This is about you, *not her*. She represents the *truth*. This energy sent a clear picture of the Holy Warrior prepared to do battle for what is right. Actually, "correct."

Hillary 1 rarely raised her center of gravity from behind the podium. She moved along precisely enunciating every word, as though she needed to be understood by one of those automated bill-paying systems. Her illustrators were generally out of sync with her message. Although it may have been her "style," it was disconcerting to watch. When she took on the role of smug Holy Warrior, she became more natural; it showed she had potential for improvement. She looked very natural while angry and thrusting her finger as she scolded her opponent.

When Hillary 2 is on topic, her body language is better than it had been previously—a remarkable transformation considering her past disconnectedness and limitations. Previously, it often looked as though someone put a recording inside a Hillary doll, and then, before she lumbered to the podium and hugged it, an aide pulled a string to make her talk. Arms moved. Head moved. Mouth moved. But nothing moved together, almost like an old dubbed Kung Fu movie.

Hillary 2 doesn't hug the podium, either, and when that changed, she got dramatically better command of a stage. Her body language still seems like she learned it as a second language and she doesn't naturally punctuate her thoughts unless she is on cause, though. Hillary 2 still has halting illustrators and awkwardness in her transitions, but she now knows what they are and how to use them. The timing just isn't there; it's like a person translating in her head.

Her stress still surfaces occasionally in a move you typically see in heavy people. It's a shifting of weight from one foot to the other in an adaptor we could call the elephant shuffle.

Another remaining flaw is that Hillary Clinton still does not have a command of the body language of honesty. She can be fiery, angry, committed, disgusted, and even amused, but she struggles to convey authenticity.

Donald J. Trump

By now you should know enough about body language to start to answer this question: What does Donald's Trump's hair suggest about his body language?

First, it is part of a brand. He is not unlike a number of other people in that strata of society, that is, less person and more product, or as Greg says, "More coat hangers and wax than person."

Secondly, the hair is a feature of an individual style that reflects the fact that he has been insulated from criticism and from mainstream society for nearly all his life. The hair, clothing, word choices, gestures, and facial expressions come together to send messages *his way*. If any of us adopted that combination of looks and sounds, we would be perceived as ridiculous. And even those who perceive *him* as ridiculous are harboring an inconsequential opinion because he doesn't care and doesn't have to care. As he joked at the end of the March 2011 Trump Roast: "What's the difference between a wet raccoon and Donald J. Trump's hair? A wet raccoon doesn't have seven billion f___ing billion dollars in the bank."[1]

As a Ringmaster, Trump has the ability to command attention and maintain control, often while he's orchestrating the moves of others around him. The quick arm movements primarily from the elbow down and commanding gestures with two open hands serve two key purposes:

1. They make Trump appear unique and larger than life; they enhance the perception of him as an 800-pound alpha. Trump is very tall for his generation and grew up in a world in which he was physically and figuratively larger than most others. He knows how to use both.

2. They reinforce his verbal game of tetherball with people he is negotiating with or debating. (Tetherball is a two-person game in which each player uses his hands or a paddle to whack a ball suspended on a rope from the top of the pole. The winner is the first person to wind the rope completely around the pole.) Many examples emerged during the Republican National Debates when Trump, as the front runner, occupied the center of the stage. When someone attacked Trump he would effectively redirect conversation and by his response push the "tetherball" to an opponent on one side or the other, at the same time bringing the opponent on the opposite side into the fray.

Trump's facial expressions are among the most complicated to read. He has developed a series of signals that those close to him can likely read very effectively, like any other gesture developed by a subculture, but watching him from a distance the complexity and variability looks odd.

Politicians and False Impressions

What do you think of Richard Nixon?

Although it isn't possible for most Americans of the Baby Boomer genera-tion, if they could watch Richard Nixon without bias, they would be charmed and surprised. They would subliminally recognize the synchronicity of his gestures and message, that is, his energy is focused in the same direction. The result is that they would perceive genuineness—until the end when he morphed into a guarded, dark individual. The Nixon who ran against John F. Kennedy, served in the White House before Watergate, and opened doors with China projected congruency and truth, and was often rather unsophisti-cated about it. His strategy was "what you see is what you get."

Now turn the prejudice around so that it works in favor of the candidate. During that presidential campaign between JFK and Nixon, the Kennedy clan moved way out front into the limelight to help his cause. His brothers were out there, and even his mother took the spotlight, ostensibly dragging Jacqueline into it, as well. They were all Holy Warriors all except for Jacqueline.

One interview that featured Rose and Jacqueline Kennedy aimed to bring the American people "into the living room" during the campaign. How that ever worked to convince average Americans that JFK should sit in the White House is testimony to our naïveté as a nation. Then, again, we still seem naïve as we browse the photographs of Donald Trump's penthouse apartment and see his 10-year-son having a normal day with his toy personalized Mercedes. Almost no one else in America lived the way the Kennedys lived, but millions of people looked up to that family and carried a bias that their "royal" pres-ence was a good thing for America—that it could lift us up. After all, if our most super-typical was so noble, what does it say about us? And is that part of a false impression we have of someone like the Kennedys and Trumps, or a valid one?

In the Kennedy interview, the two women sat on a well-upholstered, un-comfortable-looking sofa. Jackie delivered rehearsed answers to questions about the campaign—fluffy questions, not policy stuff—and Rose responded with stilted, puppet-like gestures. It was easy to wonder whose arm was in there making her head and hands do such odd things.

In another televised speech, Rose Kennedy was at a podium stumping for her son in a feather stole and pearls that were more expensive that most people's houses. Today, we would say, "What is this bull? Don't contrive things like this for us—we know better." We are a different culture now; we'd never go for the feather stole.

Pundits and Strategies

In the past decade, gender in the media has undergone some changes. Conservative pundit Ann Coulter's shrill grip on right-wing politics is no longer in fashion; the right has a different kind of sweetheart. Representative of the new kind of woman on the right are S.E. Cupp, who is geek chic, and Megyn Kelly, a fiery, yet feminine voice.

S.E. Cupp, conservative commentator for CNN, had just completed her on-air statement on May 5, 2016, that she would not be voting for Donald Trump when she was verbally attacked by pro-Trump pundit Kayleigh McEnany. Cupp batted her eyelashes in annoyance—a move that was obvious even behind her big tortoise shell glasses. She also smirked in a distinctly female style of regulator, with her lips closed in something between puckering and pursing. McEnany did a certain amount of her own lash-batting. This I'm-Just-a-Girl signaling in the days of Rumsfeld and Bush would have played to the old boy establishment to disarm the old boys. But her primary I'm-Just-a-Girl move on that show was making her eyes very big and doll-like while she spewed criticism, and that has a different impact when played out among other female pundits. The subtlety of female body language isn't lost on other women; the sudden realization that the soft fluttering of eyelashes is anything but helpless can bring out the worst in another woman.

Cupp's vigorous eyelash and eyebrow movements seem to be stock-in-trade for her. They reach a peak when she feels passionate about her topic, as in her criticism of Donald Trump when he lashed out at Fox News anchor Megyn Kelly. Host Jake Tapper asked Cupp why he would do such a thing: "I don't know why! It doesn't make a whole lot of sense!"[2] and then the eyelashes took over. But it was the shocked and censuring eyebrows that starred in her confrontation with the Trump campaign spokeswoman Katrina Pierson over Trump's proposed ban on Muslim immigration.

Fox News's Bill O'Reilly, a master of both asking questions and suggesting answers with his eyebrows, is a Holy Warrior who shows an important shortcoming in probing an "unfriendly" (that is, liberal) guest. He blockades the possibility of reading body language—and really putting some of his guests on the spot—by driving on with his prescribed agenda.

O'Reilly uses a regulator—hands up like a stop sign—to put himself back on top when he feels his guest is running away with the show. And, as we said before, he's the consummate brow-beater.

Celebrities and Strategies

Tom Cruise might strike some as a Ringmaster because of roles like Ethan Hunt in *Mission Impossible*, but when he is at his best in real life, he's a Holy Warrior. Nothing showed that more than the notorious *Today* interview with Matt Lauer on the June 23, 2005. This is the one that moved him front and center as a spokesman for the Church of Scientology, and a critic of happy drugs.

Prior to the interview turning slightly confrontational, Cruise seemed to entreat Matt Lauer to understand his points about Scientology and overuse of mood-altering medications. His hands took a position suggestive of prayer. It meant that he wanted to be understood. Before Cruise even specifically criticized Lauer for his comments on pharmaceuticals, his body started to assume the posture of someone who was going on the offensive. Just before Cruise launched into his attack on Lauer's ignorance with "you're here on the *Today* show..." his body moved into position. By the time he reprimanded Lauer for spouting off assertions without doing his homework, Cruise's body was lecturing Lauer every bit as much as his words.[3] It was an example of perfect congruency, a sign that his movements were genuine and unrehearsed. Score one for Cruise.

Mixed Messages

In an episode of *Sex and the City*, a 25-year-old female admirer of sex columnist Carrie Bradshaw asks her if she can send her something she's written. Carrie vigorously shakes her head from side to side as she says "Yes." About a minute later, the same young woman asks her if she can "assist" her. Carrie vigorously shakes her head again as she says "Yes." Carrie is a New Yorker, part of a culture unto itself; a committed head shake means, "You must be kidding. Of course not." But Carrie is too polite to let those words come out of her mouth.

Enter someone who has never rehearsed "polite": Kanye West, the Blamer. He can stir up a storm of controversy and yet not take the blame. The whole contrived feud with Taylor Swift is a great example of creating a conflict and not taking blame, but rather shifting the blame to someone else. As he struggled with Swift over her 2009 Grammy, his body language and words were pushing the blame for his actions to a friend being slighted and a cause that he had no part in. In a photo taken at the 2015 Grammy Awards with Swift—a Bubble Girl—Kanye West is smiling broadly. His mouth is slightly open and his perfect white teeth are showing, but there is no smile in the eyes. This is a deliberate mixed message shaped by sarcasm. His mind is sending the smile but his brain isn't.

Actors Playing Themselves

Before Instagram and Snapchat, we had to rely mostly on Jay Leno and David Letterman to give us a candid look at celebrities—actors playing themselves. Even now, however, late night hosts like Jimmy Kimmel and Jimmy Fallon do more to give a glimpse of how performers present their "authentic" self than social media because the hosts poke and prod in a way that often helps us catch them off guard.

A decade before writing this, we looked at Johnny Depp's body language in a July 28, 2006 interview on the David Letterman show. Almost 10 years later, on May 23, 2016, he made an appearance on *Jimmy Kimmel Live*. The conclusion is the same: It seemed apparent that Depp is, by nature, an introvert.

During both interviews, he touched his hair occasionally, scratched his head, rubbed his leg and arm, and held his crossed leg with his fingers—a leg that stayed crossed with the left ankle resting on his right thigh in the same position throughout the interview. He had a litany of adaptors.

Depp seemed genuine—his fidgeting is an expression of his true personality. So, we would conclude he was himself on the show. He didn't bother to portray a character, as many other introverted actors do when they subject themselves to late-night talk-show banter. If you ever watched late-night TV, you've seen some of those actors who try to make up for the fact that they are uncomfortable by taking on the role of entertaining guest; they come across as fake.

In contrast to Depp, Will Smith tends to be a relaxed extrovert during an interview. He easily breaks into a smile, tells self-deprecating stories, and uses his hands and arms naturally to illustrate a point. When he scratches his nose, it's probably because it itches. But even someone that comfortable with millions of eyes on him did some fidgeting in the first few minutes of his first interview on *The Tonight Show with Jimmy Fallon*. Who could blame him? He was Fallon's first guest on his first show as Jay Leno's replacement.

When actors are asked to be themselves, they often step into a challenging role.

All of the famous people we've discussed have one thing in common: They evolved a strategy by trial and error. Each of them probably started very similar to you by a simple shake of the head and a later "no" by your parents when you wanted something. Every time they met a new situation, they evolved their repertoires until the strategy was at its current state of polish. At some point we all stop polishing. The more public among us polish for longer with some of our behavioral elements "freezing" as part of our brand.

None of these survival strategies are right or wrong. What works for one person with his extroverted quick wit will not work for the systematic, thorough introvert. By now, you have enough information to analyze for yourself. For most of us, analysis of the famous is passive, meaning we will only watch body language and have little opportunity to influence the body language of the kind of people we profiled here. In the next chapter we will discuss the man in the street, so, we will start the conversation with some active use of body language or how to mange a situation using your body language to influence others.

9

The Man in the Street

You can look at "D" (decide) in two parts. The first is drawing a conclusion about what a person has done and why he has done it. The second is choosing what you want to do about that. Based on what you've determined about the person's emotional state and intent, you will either want to attract or repel that individual. In the D phase, therefore, you use the tools of R.E.A.D. intelligently and purposefully. To use a military term, you weaponize them.

Unless you observed strangers with absolutely no interaction in the review stage, you have already impacted your subjects in ways you may or may not have realized. Simply because you share a micro-culture or culture with those people, your approval or disapproval impacts their behavior and body language. Though you may not think of it as such, conversation is a form of approval or disapproval. If you didn't hide behind plants similar to some distant anthropologist during your reviews—if you behaved normally and entered into some level of discourse with those you studied—then you affected them.

Gifted conversationalists keep the flow of discussion going naturally by picking up tidbits that the other person leaks. In the interrogations world, we call this information "source leads." We all leak these facts, opinions, and reactions; they help people bond to us in conversation. If you don't do that, then you're the one at parties that no one wants to talk to. Artful conversationalists use that information to direct and manipulate the chit-chat with questions, hints, sighs, and body language.

As an exercise, stand alone at a party, but make eye contact with someone you know. Give him 30 seconds and glance again. Does the person come over to talk to you?

As the conversation starts, stay focused on the person's topic, all the while nodding your head to affirm that it's riveting. When you have gotten most of his information, start to look at your watch somewhat secretively. What happens to the conversation? Quickly explain away why you looked at the watch without divulging the real reason. Start up the conversation again. You have effectively used regulators to control the conversation. Nodding of the head makes the person think you are identifying with him and he feels validated. He will continue. A second quick glance at your watch makes the person uncertain why, but certain that you have had enough.

Although both nodding and checking your watch are regulators, the use is different. One helps you to *connect* and the other to *repel*. With practice, you can send a message with body language that you have used only passively to this point. You can set out to make your own strategies. Unlike most of the world, you will be cognizant of every move you make as part of your strategy—without the need to have someone like us analyze it for you.

Most people connect through the use of positive body language, but you can just as easily use negative behaviors to force the person to feel as though he needs your validation. You must first review his body language, evaluate what is important and different, and analyze what it means before D—deciding how to use body language. Will you use positive body language to connect with him by making him feel like a kindred spirit? Or do you notice he is an approval-seeker and determine that the negative approach through repelling motions will get him to struggle to win your approval, moving closer to you all the time?

Every interaction between humans changes the behaviors of both parties. When you are talking to someone, look for his strategies—for conflict and influence. Is it one of those listed in the last chapter, or something different? Mentally catalog these behaviors, because you will see that person use them again.

You are now moving into the sophisticated skill area of using your body language as a weapon. Be conscious of factors that will either support or degrade your efforts: filters, prejudice, lack of context, and wrong facts are a few. Just because you now know that crossing your arms does not necessarily mean you are shutting someone out, you can't presume your insight has rubbed off on other people. Most of the world does not get it; most people will make naïve assumptions and act accordingly, so use the following subtle techniques that we suggest.

Mirroring

Mirroring to gain approval or to *connect* with someone is not the monkey-like mimicking of the person's behavior. In fact, if you are a man trying to mirror a woman, the mannerisms may differ quite a bit. Mirroring means getting the gist of the other person's mannerism, so if she places a hand on her hip, you may rub your thigh slightly to get your hand in a similar position. If she puts a finger to her lips, you may brace your chin with your hand. Both are thinking gestures.

Regulators

You can use regulators to start a source down the road to compliance. Something as simple as a finger across the lips to quiet the person is a powerful request. You then read the body language to determine if it is working. Conditioned response works to your advantage and compliance with your regulator early on is a reliable sign of it. Can you always use it to arouse a subliminal sense of "I should be quiet?" Definitely not. In some cases, use it only if you are in repelling mode. Use it too obviously, and many people will see the gesture as the international symbol for "Shut the f___ up!" Be conscious of other messaging when using regulators, pay attention to your face and overall body posture, and remember that body language in all the elements is compounding. Be careful how you use it.

Adaptors

Some adaptors are best used when your subject understands a bit of body language. Tapping fingers and wringing hands send a clear message to even the least astute. One ploy is to use the tapping noise to draw a person's attention to down-right, the field of vision associated with extreme emotion, to try to agitate a person. Other adaptors that can send a clear message are rubbing the eyes, cracking knuckles, and self-grooming as a ritual of boredom. The more subtle of adaptors, such as a slight finger rub, are wasted as a tool for telegraphing because so few people recognize them for what they are. You can project discomfort, or the wish to be away from space with overt use of adaptors, but you can just as easily send the message that you are the idiosyncratic communicator and diminish the receiver's view of your message.

Barriers

Most people know a little about barriers. Remember the common—and probably your first—assumption about crossed arms? Typically, you use barriers as a tool for repelling. Most people instinctively feel shut out, and/or they feel inferior, when you use a strong barrier. Revisit the moment when you walked into your boss's office and faced a large desk. You sit exposed in a chair while the big guy builds his alpha status by sitting behind a hunk of mahogany. Real barriers are the trappings of authority.

The subtle use of barriers can message a sign of intimidation and weakness. Try crossing your arms low at your hips and holding them tightly to your body. Notice the difference in the message?

You can use your extremities or objects that you carry to barrier and, conversely, to take down the barrier to make someone feel more welcome. Contrast this experience with the first: Walk into your boss's office when she invites you to step around the barrier and review her slide presentation. Suddenly, you are on the same side. It's a very different feel from a police officer walking to the other side of his desk to close the space with a suspect; that person is not going to feel relaxed and thankful. The barrier provides a layer of protection for him. Context counts for so much in both understanding and manipulating body language—especially with barriers.

Illustrators

No one enjoys being brow-beaten during a conversation. Those Bill O'Reilly eyebrows or wagging finger of Sister Mary Obedience cause a range of negative responses from "Go away" to "I'd like to have you hauled off to the landfill."

Careful use of illustrators can repel or attract. When Hillary Clinton is "on cause" and uses her hands in an uplifting manner, brows raised and passionately talking about entitlement, she brings the crowd toward her. Open, positive use of illustrators gets the job done. When she was on target against Bernie Sanders, Hillary's opponent for the presidential nomination, her illustrators became whipping motions with her hand—brow-beating with hands instead of her eyebrows. They are repelling instruments. The key becomes a question of, "What are you trying to do: connect or repel?" Sometimes, you have to repel to get someone to bring himself closer to you. Have a plan.

Distance

Culture—from micro-culture through super-culture—dictates proximity in your interaction. In American culture, if you are intimately involved, standing far away can send a strong message of conflict. On the other hand, a casual acquaintance may be quite distressed if you move within 18 inches. Again, your intent is either to repel or connect.

How do you choose to use distance? Some people develop anti-hugger strategies to avert unwanted intrusion. The strategy may be as simple as a handshake or as complex as hand-talking that conveys, "Good to see you! We haven't seen each other in so long, we have almost become strangers." The combination of body language and words sends the message, "I like you, but feel uncomfortable with you that close." You can use your body language in this way to repel the person who is making the unwanted advance without causing hard feelings.

Timing

How quickly or slowly you respond is an indicator most people will recognize. A rushed answer can indicate urgency, especially when the answer is no. A slow answer can also be a negative when you use it intelligently. You can telegraph that you are unsure when asked for or about something by answering in a halting fashion. Women use this all the time, probably because many women are trained to be agreeable, so giving an outright "no" is uncomfortable.

"Would you like to have dinner with me?" he says.

Pause. "Well (pause), I actually have (pause) other plans," you respond. An astute man realizes you are saying, "No way in hell am I having dinner with you."

This can be a cultural phenomenon as well. Through interactions on both a personal and business level, we've seen that Mexicans are not fans of the word "no" whether it's a matter of delivering or receiving. For that reason, the communication strategies will often reflect this. In general, they will adopt strategies to avoid the topic requiring a "no" answer, or haltingly signal displeasure with the idea. When you are dealing with this you have a choice: Drive through it, or use questions to get the Mexican member of your group to tell you they do not want something. The former will not win friends as the Mexican may agree, but resent doing what you have forced upon him.

Managing Stress

Whether they do it in a calculated way or as an automatic manifestation of power, some executives use artificial stress or violation of cultural space norms to manipulate employees. When they relieve the stress, maybe by just sitting down or changing the subject, the person feels thankful to the person for relieving the stress he created in the first place.

Here's how it works in daily life: You're having lunch in a hospital cafeteria; your partner is there for routine tests. You make eye contact with someone while you deliberately put your tongue to the side of your lips, as though you were licking something that got stuck there. Watch what the person does. Chances are good that he thinks you're trying to send a message. The napkin might come up to the mouth, or depending on his cultural norm, he might wipe his mouth with his hand. You've just induced a tiny bit of stress.

Let's take a similar situation in which you ratchet up the stress even more, and then relieve it. You see someone in a crowded hospital cafeteria sitting at a table alone. You bring your sandwich over to the table, and start talking about how crowded the place is, so you're going to "borrow" the other half of the table. The person feels mildly threatened because you've invaded her space. Then you pull out your phone, say "Excuse me," and start checking your email. She now feels relieved because she realizes you have no intention of talking to her. She has no idea why she quickly feels better.

This scenario shows how you can manage stress that you created in another person. Be very careful with this kind of interaction. Either you do it with finesse, or you may be headed for conflict.

Confrontational Practices

In *Cannibals and Kings: The Origins of Cultures* (Random House, 1977), anthropologist Marvin Harris proffers four possible explanations for war. Even though he points out the reasons why each theory has holes in the anthropological big picture, the four views are salient in terms of categorizing confrontational body language, some of which is handed down generation after generation, and some of which just comes naturally. His ideas translate as well into the daily interactions of families and other micro-cultures. Unless we are talking about gang war or some such ritualistic conflict, we can assume that humans group into their armed camps in places such as office apartment buildings and even children's athletic events. The kind of warfare is simple conflict and it can range from cat-like grunts and snarls to physical violence. Consider the reasons behind it and the body language of each.

War as Solidarity

In this scenario, war results from a sense of group identity. The tribe that fights together stays together. In the modern vernacular, it's a street gang mentality. It can also be the third shift at the call center. Once you bond with other people who share your views and circumstances, you don't want to hurt your own. Aggression toward another group, even if those people share your circumstances, functions as a safety valve.

The chosen spokesperson may be super-typical, or perhaps a puppet moved to the forefront by the super-typical to confront. The purpose is to let you know that you have violated the tribe's territory. Maybe your crime is that you haven't refilled the toner in the copy machine when it was low or you took the red stapler. Regardless of cause, the body language is confrontational. If the issue is small, so is the body language, but if the issue is perceived as dire, the person's behavior may approach fight-or-flight. The gravity of the issue is dictated by the tribe's frame of reference. One common thread is the spokesperson's need for support from the group. If others are present, you may see darting eyes of uncertainty in the spokesperson as she looks for approval and reinforcement from the group—raised brows, wide open eyes as she looks at the rest of the tribe.

Movements we've seen emerge throughout the past few years like Occupy Wall Street, Black Lives Matter, Blue Lives Matter, and so on are examples of the "war as solidarity" mindset. It may be that the participants share only one idea, such as "Wall Street is about exploitation," but it's a powerful enough idea to serve as glue for people from different countries and cultures.

War as Play

Is war just a competitive, team sport? Think "football" or "reality TV." The pleasure that some people get out of taking risks simply for the adrenaline rush of putting their lives, or at least their safety, in danger is the premise behind "war as play." The additional, cultural reinforcement to repeat the performance is the reward of accolades—hero worship. The same behavior plays out every day in offices and on children's soccer fields across the United States. Confrontation as play means we have less at stake even if it falls apart and we fail we still get the rush and the conviction, "Maybe I will win next time."

The children's soccer coach gets in the face of the referee, similar to incidents occurring at the Super Bowl. Most of the time, she knows she will not win. She confronts to confront. If this were her day job, would she get in the face of her boss with her paycheck at stake? Unlike a professional athlete being ejected from the field for insolence, her rude behavior will likely not impact her income.

Who has not participated in an argument for its own sake? Why are we willing to risk losing? Because in the process we gain as well. Whether we gain status, such as the small-town lawyer who successfully confronts a big-city litigator, or simply add another layer to our personality by honing our debate skills, the allure of "war as play" is there. The danger is that we may lack assurance that the other person takes it as play as well.

In this circumstance, body language is clear. At the outset, you feel you are right and justified. People do not typically enter conflict as a game when they feel terrified of losing—unless they have self-destructive tendencies. They enter chin-up, aggressively talking, energetic, and focused.

War as Human Nature

Do human beings have a killer instinct? Does each of us have the capacity for killer behavior—or at confrontational behavior? We'll let the anthropologists slug it out over this one. What we have observed is that human beings operate on a stimulus-response basis and if the stimulus triggers an automatic aggressive reaction, even a pacifist (unless he's on par with Mahatma Gandhi) can't hold back. An interrogator will do this deliberately by synchronizing aggressive gestures and verbal attacks in an effort to bypass the source's cognitive functions, provoke his emotions, and keep going straight to his mammalian brain to get a response closest to the base as possible.

When humans enter into "war as human nature," only the most adept person can casually walk away from the outcome without long-term damage to the relationship. Interrogators use this as a tool because people will defend themselves when they feel threatened. Whether you think you have killer instinct or not, if a buff angry man gets in your face, screams and calls you a maggot, your animal self will rise up. When you go into a limbic mode, that is, reactive, you will simply respond instead of thinking. The results are clear from body language. Fight-or-flight body language surfaces: flaring nostrils, dilated pupils, elevated respiration, pale complexion, sweaty skin, tensed muscles, and grinding jaw.

In this scenario, a great deal of the body language of confrontation will be involuntary, although not necessarily universal. You might use flailing arms or clenched fists without thinking about them, but these are gestures culture has ingrained in you as signals to arouse fear in the enemy.

War as Politics

When one group attacks another to preserve or enhance its social, economic, or political interests, then war as politics comes into play. This makes particular sense if you believe that the unifying element of a culture is a shared view of quality of life, that is, what makes life good.

In some cases, what makes life good is status. Hillary Clinton and Donald Trump, as well as dozens of other people in the political arena, do this and it is played out in countless interactions in the world every day. This is the politics of jockeying for position. People go at each other until one loses. Each enters the ring with an end score in mind, and has delineated what he is willing to sacrifice to get the concession. Often, the "winner" has the least invested in the argument; he can afford to take risks because he has less to lose in the long run. He can be magnanimous in letting the other have the ostensible victory. A powerful behind-the-scenes player is less likely to engage in this kind of open warfare. Men and women will also approach this differently.

Exercise

Watch a movie in which a mix of cultures and genders engage in confrontational behavior. A number of the James Bond movies qualify. Or tune into one of the reality shows that forces people from different backgrounds into a common dilemma. Sort the body language by culture and gender. One way to tell if something is distinctly cultural is to envision someone with a different background using the same gesture. Would it not have the desired effect or be funny instead of threatening? A good example is the pre-attack stance of a martial arts expert and the accompanying "Hi-ya!" You won't run away if Chris Rock does it in his comic, mocking style.

Open your eyes to the verbal and non-verbal conversations that go on around you. How much interaction occurs? How much of it is intentional? In the words of Carl Jung: "The meeting of two personalities is like the contact of two chemical substances: if there is any reaction, both are transformed."

Tread carefully on your acquaintances.

10

Using Body Language to Your Advantage in Business

Business is a subset of the rest of humankind. Think of it as a micro-culture or sub-tribe composed of people from multiple tribes who come together for a common purpose. Whether you are the receptionist or the CEO, you are part of a collective that shares a reason for being at work. In this process, you have to learn the social norms of others. Even if you are the super-typical, you still need to follow certain ground rules. You can change these through precedent, but even then, there are limits. Greg has completed six major business transformation initiatives that include massive change, but throughout those significant experiences, he still has to live by the "rules" regardless of endorsement, position, or backing. Businesses can effortlessly smother any initiative by intruders.

We start with this discussion because you need to be conscious of what the ground rules are for your tribe. Unacceptable behavior may get you voted off the island. Your first step is to assess the tribe.

Assess

Who are the super-typical at work? Are they all formally appointed leaders or, like an insurgent group, are there also sleepers (stealth super-typical people whose influence outstrips their pay)? We will look at why that's important to know before examining how you can identify them.

Some people in the super-typical category get there by appointment or promotion, and then work all the way to the top. Achievement drives them. The alpha often has an I-love-me wall, an Army-ism for a place a person puts all his awards and achievements. Everyone can sense this alpha's importance from body language, and the body language of others around him, so the situation is easy to see and easy to manage.

Other super-typical people in the organization may be less visible, but are just as important. Let's call this group the *stealth-heroes*.

The Influence Peddler

The influence peddler sits behind the throne, perhaps without an official title, but with a network of associates who trust him and seek his advice. When she decides to heft her influence, she can make or break a project, timeline, or budget. She may only have the king's (or queen's) ear through complaints, but her power is vast. Unless the queen removes her, the queen must consult with the influence peddler to reach the masses. In corporate acquisitions, this is particularly difficult since the acquiring company must be respectful of the "elders" of the purchased business. Whether it's the mom-and-pop owners of a small business, or key people in a large corporation, they are the local leaders. They may have a formal or an informal designation, but they are the super-typicals. Leave them in power too long, and you risk lack of assimilation of the new business. Remove them too quickly, and you risk mass exodus or loss of engagement. Even decades later, employees of an acquired company may refer to themselves as "the old Kmart guys," or something similar. The influence peddlers in these organizations are well-rooted and wait out change effectively.

The Advisor

Whether trusted by the king because he has saved his hide before, or simply because the king feels they are like-minded, he is the confidant of leadership. A difficult person to read because he may have no outward opinions, he is the most dangerous of the informal leaders: Discrediting him means discrediting the king himself. Why was President Obama so fiercely protective of his Secretary of State Hillary Clinton? It called his judgment into question if the media was allowed to beat up Clinton. The advisor on the positive side is aware of this power and uses it for the good of the company because he has clout with others. On the negative side, he becomes a monster as he constantly uses the threat of his power.

The Instigator

The instigator holds no power, either official or otherwise. His only power is to stir up trouble. When displeased, he can cause things to go awry, and may not have the ability to undo the damage. In some cases, it is because he is a well-liked typical; in others, a quirky super-typical. And in yet others, he is the crazy uncle—but he's "our" crazy uncle through tenure at the organization. In any event, his importance centers on his ability to derail your plans, so you need to read his body language for signs of irritation. Killing off the instigator does no good. The micro-culture will spawn another just like him. Your best opportunity is to co-opt him.

The Coalition Builder

This first-cousin of the instigator also cannot exist without strife. She finds a way to compromise all of the groups and convince them that they are happy with the outcome. The most successful coalition builders manipulate with ease and either cause the strife themselves or allow it to fester until it reaches a point at which all parties must come together. She talks about everyone winning, which is easy for her to say, because she is the only one truly getting what she wants: resolution. The other parties lose in some way. She often skirts personal conflict, preferring to point out that she isn't the problem, but rather the solution. Nonetheless, she may point constantly to the problem. She may even invent the problem from a series of symptoms and is ever-ready to help "everyone come to a solution."

The Royal Cousin

The figure of authority by association plays out in many different ways. They all have one thing in common and that is a misplaced sense of authority. Whether it is in the context of the military (the brother of a commander acting like a bigshot), or in business (an employee whose husband is the president of another company thinking she must be important, too), people mistake status in one relationship to equal power in another. This can also play out with a person in a corporate support role in a U.S.-owned company trying to direct a person senior to her in a foreign division because she feels closer to the company's intent. It is flawed logic in each case, but if unchecked it is *de facto* power and it happens all the time in business.

■　■　■　■　■

The categories describe a select number of roles; you may have noticed others. This is your tool set; now create your own set of stealth-heroes. Next you need to learn how to uncover and deal with these stealth-heroes. Keep these things in mind as we go through the process:

- One person may fill multiple roles, or have solid identification with a single one.

- The roles assumed by an individual may progress. For instance, an influence peddler/instigator may become the advisor simply because the alpha wants to keep him as close as possible for greater scrutiny.

The instigator is the easiest to spot. While others suffer over the latest mayhem, he shows smug pleasure—chin up, eyes comfortably open—as he surveys the outcome of his latest venture with a glow of righteous indignation. Maybe even a smirk and prolonged eye contact as he watches his work. Some instigators are loud and obstinate. These will typically only behave this way when they have someone in a compromising situation, such as ill-prepared for a meeting or short on fulfilling the terms of an agreement. The instigator will rarely launch a headlong attack against someone who is prepared, which makes him similar to a hyena rather than a lion.

Most work behind the scenes and have the body language of secretiveness. They may instigate by sharing information or asking questions that get others to uncover the facts. The best way to combat the instigator is to have him publicly endorse you, as in "keep your friends close, and enemies closer." Once the instigator endorses you—and this "declaration" may be solely in the form of body language that clearly realigns his relationship with you—he runs the risk of losing his credibility if he attacks you or backs away. You have something to hold over him with his co-conspirators. You have the key to causing public humiliation.

The advisor can be spotted rather easily. This golden-haired child has gained the confidence of the king, so he can place his words directly into the king's ear. This has occurred either because the king fears his power or identifies with him. There are two types:

1. The "you're like me" advisor. You cannot win a head-to-head confrontation with an advisor in front of others without first pointing out that he is very different from the alpha. Disgracing him is a direct assault on the alpha, after which the advisor can just step away and watch you fall. The only way to win the argument is one on one, or by first separating him from the alpha; that is, divide and conquer. This can come about by playing instigator in open meetings: You ask questions that spotlight the differences to clarify the point to alpha. And then, once the alpha starts to ask the questions, you wait for the fireworks.

2. The "I'm keeping you close for scrutiny" advisor. Already suspicious of this advisor, the alpha is constantly watching his back. You win in open confrontation with this advisor by waiting him out and asking questions that will force the hand of the alpha. The alpha cannot sit idly by as the advisor spouts rhetoric counter to the alpha's thoughts. Here's an example: A manager who understands the CEO's priority to boost the bottom-line has a good chance of putting a CIO into the closet if the CIO's plan to standardize software in the company undermines that manager's ability to make a profit.

The influence peddler is the rock on which the company is built. Everyone owes her something, including you, whether or not you perceive it. She keeps a list and checks it twice. Easy to spot, she is the social butterfly of the organization. In the classic TV show *M*A*S*H*, he is Sergeant Luther Rizzo, the motor pool sergeant, who sells stolen oil to get eggs for the chow hall so Hawkeye can produce an omelet to seduce the pretty nurse so Rizzo can secretly acquire Penicillin to treat his venereal disease. This is energy-intensive. Maintaining all of those relationships is similar to spinning plates on poles. Because of that, the person is nimble in conversation, but less likely to take the limelight. You will notice the influence peddler by preoccupation. The way to defeat her is to become the most important cog in the wheel. Identify the keystone of her influence and gently insert yourself into that position. The result is that she is no longer important without your cooperation.

You only get close to this person with the body language of helplessness—arms open, concerned brow, needy posture—as you ask how you can resolve your problem. You will see their acts of magnanimity as they extend arms and enlighten you.

The coalition builder is easy to spot because he is always helpful. Listen to him walk down the halls whistling his win-win tune. He moves adeptly between the opposing forces of the armed camps within the organization. Typically, he has the ability to see both sides of the coin and is not overly connected to either. He brokers arrangements, which are pure genius in compromise terms. The reason is simple: He loses nothing in the deal, so the win-win is his win. He sells the fact that he can create a truce and he does so by creating a solution in which both of the opposing parties lose some, but not all. King Solomon's ploy to determine the real mother of a baby was the ultimate coalition-builder move. (For those who are weak on Bible stories: Two women claimed they were the mother of the same baby. He said he would split the baby in half, which one woman agreed to, but the other asked simply that the baby be allowed to live.) Solomon, of course, resolved his dilemma more wisely than most by doing the right thing while exhibiting utter brilliance. The coalition builder is always the real winner in the situation. Opposing him is dangerous because the solution he represents is the one that makes the alpha happy.

The way to defeat the coalition builder is by having him identify with your cause as he describes his solution. At that point, if his solution has the potential to damage your cause, then his strategy becomes self-defeating. This is a difficult ploy because most coalition builders will have nothing vested in any outcome other than the alpha's desired one. Maryann once saw this play out in a silly company fight over a logo. One faction wanted the logo in blue, and the other, red. The coalition builder knew that his boss preferred red, but someone from the blue faction casually caught the ear of the coalition builder: "Maybe red really is better. It's eye-catching. I mean, you see it on stop signs, police cars—it really makes you take notice." As soon as the coalition builder mentioned stop signs and police cars to the boss, he found lots of reasons to get people to rally around the blue. The coalition builder supported blue fully from then on.

So far, everything we have talked about in this chapter is similar to intrigue out of *The Prince* or *Dangerous Liaisons*, but it need not be. Can a skilled person use these tactics when in the presence of harsh negotiators? Yes. However, the preferred route is the straight-forward approach.

Shut Up

In a room full of experts, you can appear to know more about a subject than others if you sit long enough and listen. Here are the steps:

- Watch body language and illustrators. That tells you what really matters to other people in the room.

- Collect information from others and sort it into people, events, timing, location, and other key sorting factors.

- At the end of two hours of wrangling, you should have what you need to begin the distillation process. You are in a position to boil down the issues to the things all of you have said and agreed on, but not heard.

By following these steps, you can suddenly appear to have the whole issue wrapped up. Imagine the control you could exercise with an immense amount of knowledge about a subject if you applied the same technique.

Never Argue When You Are Wrong, Unless For Sport

If you play the devil's advocate for sport, you may take a losing side just to sharpen your skills. Otherwise, losing an argument sets a precedent. If you win every argument, you seem to have secret powers.

How can you possibly win if you frequently argue when you are wrong? Only rarely would you want to engage in conflict for sport in the workplace. If you happen to be a professional negotiator it may boost your stock, but for the rest of us, it is just dangerous. You may find yourself in the middle of an argument on the losing side without wanting to be there, though. At that point, read the body language of your opposing party and any other witnesses. How do they perceive the contest? Is there a smirk of self-confidence in your opponent? Do the spectators support you or him? Do you notice a hands-on-hips gesture that projects his confidence?

Noticing behavior similar to this, you need to choose your response based on the type of person he is: alpha, hidden, super-typical, stealth-hero, or typical. You could respond by giving up and, depending on the circumstances, walking away. Or you could regain a measure of stature by waiting until you can make at least one point that shakes his confidence. While he is tabulating his answer, concede so as to leave doubt in his and others' minds.

Never Argue and Lose in Public

Never voluntarily argue with someone in public. Not only is it undignified to argue with a subordinate, if he happens to make you look stupid, it's potentially tragic for you. Also, never argue with a boss in public, because either you look stupid or he looks stupid and you suddenly look unemployed.

Unless no other option seems to exist, keep arguments behind closed doors in a business setting. When forced to get confrontational in public, you can use dirty tricks involving body language or interrogation ploys, such as attacking the person's pride or ego to get him into a position of compromise.

("Someone as bright as you could not have meant that.") You may even want to resort to a little duck-season/rabbit-season logic shift to make your opponent look bad. For those of you who were deprived of Bugs Bunny, it simply means using the person's reasoning reworded to make him attack his own logic. When the argument is a matter of opinion, just push him to rage and nothing looks as dim-witted as rage.

Catch Flies With Honey

The best use of these body-language tools in business is as an aid to understanding the real message someone is trying to get across. You can use them to create, rather than destroy, relationships, and they allow you to navigate more effectively among warring parties.

You are developing the skills to see what lies beneath—to understand what a person is feeling, but not saying. Use that to reach the person on a deeper level and understand the issue from her perspective.

Talk About the Elephant in the Room

When someone's body language screams, "I have a problem with you," but his mouth is saying, "Everything is fine," he secretly wants to get the problem out in the open. No one likes that feeling of pent-up frustration. The person will feel better about you for addressing the issue. People feel strangely obligated to those who relieve stress, even if they are the source of the stress.

Read the Pauses and Rushes

People leave pauses in awkward places and rush statements as a way of asking you to delve deeper. They may not be doing it on a conscious level, but these stops and starts are a request just the same. Listen for the non-verbal clues and look for the request-for-approval body language that says, "Are you going to let me get away with that?" or "You do believe me, don't you?" Look for a request for approval and raising of the brow to indicate an opening to conversation.

Use the Inclination of Humans to Social Norming

Chapter 2 touched on the nature of humankind. The more often you conduct a meeting that is successful and everyone feels as though they are a valued participant, the more invested they become in your culture. People do not go to war against people similar to themselves. You do not need some guru to have you participate in a trust exercise to create a cohesive unit. The alpha sends the norms.

Look for Patterns of Behavior

Some patterns of behavior roll down from the top of the mountain and others sprout from the ground. Observe your corporate micro-culture so you know where the social norming starts.

Does your company have homesteaders (cubes that remind you of home) or crypt dwellers (stone cold, no photos or personal effects)? These external signs can be great indicators of the thoughts of people in your company, particularly whether or not they have a sense of trust and relationship with people. Does their body language reinforce your conclusion?

Be Honest

A refreshing change, and a side effect, of you understanding body language is that you will be hypersensitive to your own behavior when you lie. You will notice every unplanned pause and wrong accessing cue. You will see yourself barriering when you do not want to be discovered. The stress can be unbearable.

Life is much easier after you know this. You will be predisposed to keep communication straightforward and honest. There is another one of those social norms we told you we would implant as a result of you reading this book.

By the way, the honesty we refer to here is common-sense honesty, not the radical honesty that compels you to tell your wife she looks awful with her new haircut.

Your body language skills will not work office magic, or any other kind. Their advantage, which may seem to others like magic, is that you can know what the whole organism is saying. Every culture or micro-culture is its own, evolving organism. By watching the members of the hive you can see changes to the culture.

11

Using Body Language in Your Personal Life

The term "personal life" encompasses a broad spectrum of relationships. If you are married or in a committed relationship you have a solid set of rules and expectations created by your two-person micro-culture. If you are reading this because you think your partner violated one of your entitlements, we will tell you upfront: There are ways to use body language in a passive fashion to get the truth. However, if you are looking for the kind of Machiavellian tools covered in the business chapter so you can use them on your partner, you will not find those here.

Non-Complementary Behavior

Before going into specific areas of your personal life, such as dealing with pushy sales people or first dates, we want to explore a concept that is useful in all of them. It builds on the concept of meta-behaviors, that is, the mirroring and rituals that influence body language.

Consider how a person born and raised in Northern New Jersey—yes, we're going with the stereotype of someone who is very expressive—might act if someone let a door shut in his face. The absolutes would surface: the facial expression that's easily identifiable as anger and accompanying illustrators that punctuate what we see on the face. But in addition, after this person goes through the doorway, he might slam the door behind him to catch the attention of the offender. The action is a way to say, "You did something to piss me off and I'm going to let you know how I feel about that." The ritual here is that *every time* someone does something to aggravate him, he would take a similar retaliatory action. He would stomp, throw something, or slam a door.

The person who is guilty of letting the door fly into this guy's face might respond in a normal way. He sees the anger in the face and mirrors it. His back goes rigid, he clenches his fists a little, and he returns the negative emotion. This is an example of *complementary behavior*, or *complementarity*—the behavior we commonly have with another person, whether we know the person or not. You are pleasant to me and I am pleasant to you. You grumble at me, I grumble at you. It's basic mirroring, as in "monkey see, monkey do."

Non-complementary behavior runs counter to that. Mahatma Gandhi and Martin Luther King famously returned hateful words with gentle ones, and violent actions with demonstrations of peace. There is no guarantee that such non-complementary behavior will diffuse a situation, but the ability to mirror, which we have because of our mirror neurons, gives us the ability to read a person's mood. If we carefully observe and listen, we can figure out if non-complementary behavior is an appropriate strategy at the moment.

It had been 20 years since Greg was in a car accident, but with a convergence of things going wrong on the road, he rear-ended a car driven by a middle-aged woman. She jumped out of the car screaming at Greg about how stupid he was. The severity of her response far exceeded the fender-bender circumstances and culminated in a personal accusation: "Why would you do this to me?!" Greg concluded that her reaction was beyond the bounds of normalcy, so there must be something else going on. He reached out and hugged her. As she started to cry, the anger left her body. She said she was going through a horrible divorce and this was her husband's car.

Greg's non-complementary behavior was less of a gamble for him than it would be for most people because of his expertise in reading people, so rather than making this the default in a tense situation, use the skills you're developing here to assess the person first. Of course, there are many non-tense, day-to-day situations in which non-complementary behavior could be useful to shifting the mood of the moment—and perhaps the result. As we go through the various types of interactions you might have in your daily life, think about how behavior that doesn't mirror the other person's might help you achieve your goal.

Sales

This is your body-language primer on dealing with salespeople or others who intrude into your arena. The best and pushiest salespeople, such as those timeshare folks, are usually reasonably good at instinctively doing what's discussed in this book.

When you do not want the intrusion of a fundraiser, salesman, or door-to-door evangelist, use the combined body language of barriering that says, "I do not have time for you":

- Crossed arms.
- Looking at your watch.
- Expressionless face.
- Little to no eye contact.

The message this combination sends is clear: "Go away." Of course, you could simply say "I'm not interested" and close the door, but most Americans have a difficult time being that abrupt; we have a difficult time saying no. That is the second part of our complex personalities that we learn from our parents. After they teach us through positive reinforcement that shaking our heads will cause them to stop feeding us, then they teach us *no* is the word we say to stop doing something. As soon as we master *no*, however, they glare and say "Don't say 'no' to me!" The message stays with us our entire lives.

All of the behaviors mentioned in the previous bullets could be considered non-complementary behavior, by the way. Instead of mirroring the salesperson by having open body language, actively listening to the pitch, smiling occasionally, and looking right at him, you've flipped the behaviors 180 degrees.

Car Dealer

A car dealer is a different breed of salesman. Nearly no one goes to a car dealer casually, without intent. Knowing that, he uses the spider-to-the-fly invitation. He moves in for the kill when he sees the body language of excitement or interest. This is not meant to imply that this skill reflects dishonesty. Some dealers genuinely want to serve your need for personal mobility. Others prey on those who know the least and take the role of advisor by becoming the expert. They tout safety features to new mothers and horsepower to young men. The trick with this behavior is to project what you want him to see and feign interest down several tracks to get him to use everything in his repertoire.

By doing this, you will know him inside-out before you sit at the table to discuss money. Once you sit, you will see familiar gears engage. He will try to maneuver, usually from behind a barrier. He will turn the contract around to you. Look at it for a few seconds. Use phrases such as, "From where I am sitting," or "If you were sitting here, you would see what I mean" to suggest that he really would benefit in this deal if he understood your point of view. At the same time, use your body language to get him from behind the desk. Now he is in your court and you can negotiate more effectively.

Dealing With High Pressure

Not all salespeople are high pressure, nor do all high-pressure tactics come from salesmen. Fundraisers, evangelists, people desperate for a date, and even friends, family members, and acquaintances can resort to high pressure to get what they want. This pressure usually involves some sort of bonding behavior that makes the person similar to you and makes it more difficult for you to say no to this fellow tribe member.

As a literary agent, Maryann gets calls and emails every week from wanna-be authors. They often try to arouse a sense of connection, as in, "We went to the same university" or "I grew just 20 miles from your hometown." The theory is a good one: They think the more they are perceived as part of the same tribe, the better their chances are for being accepted as a client. Recently, an author called and, after introducing himself, promptly expressed condolences regarding a mutual friend who passed away. Maryann didn't know this author, but the emotional response to the loss of her friend was hard to quell: "Yes, she was very dear to me and I miss her so much." The author then proceeded to pitch his latest book in the hope that he would get an immediate offer of representation. Fortunately, Maryann has a policy of not making such an offer without reviewing the material first. If the Pope called, she might rethink that policy, but for now, it saves her from losing the distance she needs to make a good business decision.

Although this pressure was on the phone, the same rule applies when dealing with high pressure in person. You have more signals and can read the person's intent and veracity more clearly, but the full-bodied press is harder to resist. If you do not know the person's baseline, ask questions and R.E.A.D. Those questions must be stress-free so you can ascertain what she does, how she speaks, and where her eyes move while you simply chat. If you know the baseline, look for indicators. If the person is family or a real friend (more on that later), and in need of the requested amount or favor, sometimes personal sacrifice is in order. Do not just give in, though. You have the tools for uncovering need versus want.

When you decide you are not willing to give in or give up, use the momentum of the requestor against him. He has specific expectations that "x" will work. Let him think it is working, all the while nodding until you can see a flaw in the reasoning, and then point it out. The result is he has gone too far down one track to reverse course without loss of credibility. Most people will leave you alone at this point.

Friend or Acquaintance

This is the hardest distinction to make, primarily because of all the microcultures affecting us. Whether it is a friend or acquaintance, we clearly share at least one micro-culture with the person, and each one adds layers of complexity to our personalities. Whether or not you're a hugger, many people are. To them, hugging signals closeness and expresses joy in seeing a friend. But for some people, hugging seems bizarre. Differences in upbringing and experiences in life make us who we are. To confuse a reluctance to hug with a lack of affection would be tragic.

When an issue similar to this arises, ask yourself: Does he care about what is going on in your life? We don't mean the details of your life, but about your general well-being, like what is making you lose sleep and what is making you happy. You can read body language well enough now to tell genuine interest from perfunctory displays. On the other hand, a woman who is only interested in what keeps you awake at night may not be so interested in your overall well-being. R.E.A.D. Use everything you know and overlay gender, culture, and context to decide for yourself.

The other question you might ask yourself is: "How long can I go without seeing this person before something changes in the way I am treated the next time I see her?" If the answer is "Not long," then she is an acquaintance.

Dating

How do you approach someone you find attractive and determine whether or not she is available and interested? Some seem to have a natural gift for detecting this; others have the mating instincts of rocks. As a young soldier, Greg worked with another soldier who was extremely good looking. He might have been able to attract any woman he met if he'd only kept his mouth shut. Women walked away from him because crass and stupid don't appeal to most women. From a man's perspective, he was a good guy to hang out with because he was a chum. Not *a* chum, but the stuff you throw into the water to attract sharks. His good looks drew women in, and his buddies could close the deal.

To do this, R.E.A.D. to determine whether you are hitting or missing the mark in your conversation. Using the same skill set covered in the business chapter, simply watch for stressors in the person's speech and body language to find out where her passion is. If she hates something, and so do you, that is a better place to start the conversation than "Come here often?" You may not, in fact, have anything in common, but you can start the conversation by at least appearing to care that she hates avocados. Mirror body language to make the person feel closer to you, but do it in a way that is consistent with you in terms of gender and culture. If you don't do "soft" well, then don't try to pull it off.

The next step you take is reading body language for signs of acceptance, if not attraction. You already know the basics for acceptance:

- The opening of space to you.

- Body language supporting verbal messages.

- Timing and distance that signal "positive," that is, using body language to connect as opposed to repel you.

When you actually have a connection and there is sexual interest, your behavior should be in synch with your mood. Males have more of a tendency to speak quieter. Both men and women will have more blood flow to the mucosa, resulting in fuller lips and flushed cheeks. The pupils dilate to draw in more of a good thing. Both men and women may slow the rate of speech to be softer and more appealing. Unconscious mirroring becomes rampant. As a test to see where you are, consciously introduce an inconspicuous movement just to see if it is mirrored. If so, you have a green light.

Committed Relationships

Many committed relationships start on faulty ground. There are no clearly defined expectations or entitlements. Most arguments, fights, and hard feelings result from one or both of the parties feeling these undefined entitlements have been violated. In fact, it is an expectation. When this happens, because the committed relationship is likely the most emotional of our lives, the starting point of the exchange takes on an explosive quality. Remember: One of the thickest filters to see through is emotion. If you can back away from the emotional component and use the techniques we have taught you here, you can rise up to a level of success that will surprise you.

Given that every relationship is a micro-culture, you have developed rituals and subtleties of body language with your partner that are so obscure, no one else may notice. Your mate projects squarely what that raised eyebrow means when aimed at you. In some cases, perhaps the thought is very different from what it meant in the last fight—maybe the eyebrow is raised and there is a distracted half-smile. The review skills you've been honing will help you see that.

We all have trigger points that arise from years of baggage with a person who is very close to us. To take your new brush and paint over old wallpaper would be absurd and unproductive. Use the tools first to understand. If you employ your skills in a ground-up way, you might actually notice something good rather than bad.

Turn 180 degrees. You want to use the tools to understand because you suspect something is amiss. Start with baselining.

- Where do his eyes go when he discusses what he wants to do on vacation this year? If they go to the same place when you ask him where he was at 2 p.m. yesterday, you likely have cause for concern. Why? The first answer should be creative and the second one should be memory, with the eyes signaling access on difference sides of the brain.

- Does his tone, cadence, posture, or barriering change when you get near a topic you are concerned about? If so, there is another cause for concern.

One final thing to remember is that your eyes are jaundiced by emotion if you have gotten to this point. You will have a hard time being truly objective. (For a deeper explanation about deciphering such behavior, we go into much more detail in *How to Spot a Liar*.)

The best opportunity to get the truth is to use your own projected body language to express genuine concern and remind the person that you are part of the same tribe. Show that you matter, and that lying to you or mistreating you is painful. If you can come across as forgiving and willing to listen and identify with your partner, you may get the person to confess his or her violation of your entitlement. If it is something big, then at least you have a factual basis for deciding on a course of action. Something small? Establish clearer expectations so that it never becomes something big.

We cannot say this often enough: Body language skills are not party tricks; they offer you a serious ability to improve communication and operate more effectively in all kinds of environments. Do not inflict your new tools on people around you. You will only make them nervous and possibly resentful.

Part IV:
Conclusion

12

Case Study: Is Lee Harvey Oswald's Death a Conspiracy?

To conclude our course in R.E.A.D., we thought we would review the meaning of an infamous event. It's a way to drive home key points as well as entertain your iconic mind. Let's discuss and dissect a classic incident in history. You decide whether or not there was a conspiracy based on the body language evidence. We point out the "R," "E," and "A" and let you fill in the "D."

This question is not whether there was a conspiracy to kill President John F. Kennedy. The question is: Was killing Lee Harvey Oswald, accused assassin of Kennedy, an intentional, planned act of conspiracy, or the act of a rogue assassin?

Look at the image of Oswald's shooting just prior to Jack Ruby firing the bullet. What do you see? A vigilante shooting an assassin? A police department set up to eliminate with extreme prejudice the same suspect? What do the elements of R.E.A.D. suggest to you?

Digitally re-mastered video posted on YouTube captures the Oswald shooting (*www.youtube.com/watch?v=3n9VQ-dXrwQ*). Watch the very short video while you keep the "R" in mind.

Pretend for just a minute you do not know the outcome. Or if you have never been exposed to this key incident from United States history, then the exercise has an added dimension for you. Just watch the video (and others), which opens with an interview of Oswald in which he is asked about his guilt or innocence. It will allow you to get a sense of certain things that were normal for media interviews and law enforcement interviews in 1963.

© AP

Review

The Stage

The action takes place in the basement of a Dallas police station.

- Was it an iconic setting for you, or was it ordinary in the sense that it represented nothing particular?
- Does it impact your sense of safety for the victim?
- Does anything about the setting hold specific meaning for you, from the depth of the hallway to the bare bricks of the wall?
- What is the impact to the actors?
- Is the staging intentional for some and incidental for others?

The Blocking

- How do the actors—reporters, policemen, Lee Harvey Oswald, Jack Ruby (when he enters the scene), media representatives—present themselves and interact?
- Does anything look planned?
- What looks "normal"?
- Did the actors look like their movements were programmed in three dimensions, plus time, to indicate planning and or rehearsal?
- Did it look like anyone was about to deliver a line or take an action?
- Did any element of their behavior look like bad acting?

The Costumes

- Did any clothing immediately stand out, or did it seem ordinary?
- Is it important that Oswald's clothing is markedly different from those around him?
- Does anyone's clothing engender trust?
- Does anyone's clothing put you off or seem out of place?

The Props

- Do you notice anything odd in the surroundings that set the stage? For example: There is someone who appears to be a reporter who is holding a microphone near him rather than aimed at Oswald. Did he really want an interview?

- Did any of the set props impact your thoughts or feelings?

- What about the rifle and the fact it was "foreign made"? Did that affect you? What do you think it did to the people in the video?

- Were any of the props stimulus for the actors, meaning did anything look out of place or placed there for a reason?

- Considering *The Big 5* plus all the signals we have discussed from scalp to sole, what do you see?

The Players

- Who are the "actors" in this scene? Twenty-two men are visible in this photo. Some are in the rear shadows, but they are, nonetheless, part of the scene.

- Are they all relevant?

Verbal Indications

- Is anything out of the ordinary in the conversation?

- Is anyone using jargon or odd language that isn't obvious without "insider" information?

Vocal Indications

- Are tone and pitch appropriate for the actors? Police? Reporters? Oswald?

- What about cadence? Does anyone seem particularly nervous or oddly calm?

Gestures

- Are there any gestures you recognize?

- Are there gestures that you do not recognize, but someone else appears to, certainly those that would occur in a secretive operation?

- Do you see any signaling that went on between the actors that also had the body language of recognition? Look carefully because you do not need to understand the signaling to know if two people are doing it. Be aware of the body language of secrecy, like signaling with hands between gang members.

Adaptors

- Is anyone showing discomfort (outside of a situational level of discomfort)?
- Is anyone doing something that looks like self-comforting and out of place? Does it fit the situation?

Illustrators

- Are the actors who are talking punctuating their thoughts in a natural way?
- Are there people illustrating their thoughts without moving their lips?

Regulators

- Is anyone containing, speeding, slowing, or controlling who does what in the verbal and non-verbal conversation?
- Are there unspoken, formal regulators, that is, restraints that fit the situation, but alter the conversation?
- Are there any that do not fit the situation?

Barriers

- Does anyone have an artificial barrier real or other?
- Is it appropriate for the situation?
- Is it timed correctly?

Ekman's Absolutes

- Do you see any of the seven expressions of emotion? (This doesn't take more than a glance at the faces.) Make note of which player is expressing which emotion. Don't worry about whether it means anything yet.

Meta-behaviors

- In this short video you probably will not pickup on mirroring; if you do, note it. Was it intentional? Or was it adaptational (that is, a survival tool)?

■ ■ ■ ■ ■

Your catalog of movements and sounds should be complete. You have a lot of information about the setting, as well as the actors and their basic body language. Time to start E.

Evaluate

Mood

What was the mood of each actor? Remember to look at the three elements of mood: energy, direction, and focus. Make note of the mood of each of the actors using this table.

- Does the table capture the moods? Is it something else? Create your own.

Mood	Energy	Direction	Focus
Confusion	Low	Scattered	Internal
Distraction	High	Scattered	Internal
Anger	High	Sharp	External
Joy	High	Sharp	External
Excitement	High	Scattered	Stimulus dependent
Interest	High	Sharp	External
Fear	High	Sharp	External
Secretiveness	Low	Sharp	External
Embarrassment	Low	Sharp	Internal

- What impact did the particular mood have on the body language of the other actors?
- Since you have a head full of mirror neurons, what impact did their moods have on you?

Explore "Normal"

What is normal for the culture depicted in the video? This is the 1960s in the United States, specifically in an urban area of Texas. A few cultural nuances have changed in the decades since then.

Stage: In the early 1960s, imagery by video was not the norm. News footage shot outside a studio like this film of a prisoner transfer isn't nearly up to today's standards. It's grainy and ill-lit. Speculate that this might have even been the first time a prisoner transfer was filmed in Dallas. The area was likely not conducive to filming since it wasn't the primary purpose of the facility and not a common occurrence.

The relationship between reporters and law enforcement officers was not as strained as today and many cops and reporters knew each other well.

The Miranda Supreme Court ruling requiring suspects to hear their rights occurred in 1966—three years after the Oswald incident—so the legal counsel that Oswald is requesting was not yet on the tips of every American's tongue. Rights of the accused were conveyed differently.

The politeness of American culture, whether tongue-in-cheek or real, was very different from today. People lacking intimate familiarity with each other used titles like "mister" instead of first names. Add to all of these facts the reality that this is occurring in the Deep South, that is, where cultural elements we characterize as "Southern" have a pervasive influence on customs and even behavior. Given these factors, what do you see that looks out of the norm for a stage?

Blocking

- How should this interview look? Planned? Spontaneous? This is arguably the highest profile murder of the 20th century.
- How should the subject be protected? Restrained? Allowed to Speak? Questioned?
- Where should members of the public be in regards to an accused assassin?

- Do the movements look routine, or just the opposite? In other words, whose actions look intentional and normal for the situation, and whose seem to be stimulus-based within the situation?
- Do the officers look like it is routine for them, though not for others?
- How does Oswald look in the video?
- What about the reporters in the video: Do they move like this event has generated energy for them?
- Do they look anxious to get images?
- Are they moving to get normal imagery?
- Are they inserting themselves to get closer before they lose an opportunity due to the transport arriving?
- Is that "normal" considering the situation, or is it awkward and ostensibly choreographed beforehand?
- Do they appear to know the shooter is coming?
- If so, wouldn't they wait for just the shot?
- Do the officers look surprised by the shot?
- In the still image, the officers appear to be offering up the assassin. Does that change when you see the blocking in motion?
- If anyone appears to be abrupt, rushed, and planned, who is it?
- When the shooter arrives do the police look like they are doing what you would expect, that is, do they simply stand or are they reacting? And is whatever they are doing appropriate? More importantly, how do they move—like a plan?
- What is the mood?
- Look at the others around the action: What is their reaction? Now compare this to the body language of the people who would be in on the action—the officers—if this were a conspiracy.
- Are the officers moving differently and showing different body language from the bystanders? If so, is it because of their profession? Is that normal compared to earlier baseline?

Individuals

- Now go out and look at the individual non-verbals you cataloged. Does anything stand out as out of the norm?
- Are individuals acting dramatically different from the norms of the group they are part of?

Look at *The Big 5* and the scalp-to-sole you listed. What is abnormal in that list? Weave in the elements listed in the "E" exercise so far. Just evaluate the normal from the abnormal, taking into account the mood and situation. Look to see how culture impacts the signaling, and then look for what is abnormal even within that group. For example, the culture of law enforcement involves norming certain behaviors that are almost as iconic as the badge.

Almost ready to decide? First let take a look at a few things you might be projecting on to the group before we rush that decision.

Analyze

- Did you notice that everyone in the images is middle-aged, white, and male?
- What is the impact?
- Do you immediately trust or mistrust them?
- Is it because of a simpler time in your mind? Or a racist Southern police force?
- Did you hear Oswald ask for representation? How many times?
- Does that impact your trust in the police force?
- As we referenced previously regarding guiding your evaluation, it wasn't until 1966 in Miranda v. Arizona that the Supreme Court decided that a suspect's words were admissible during a trial only if the prosecution could show that he was told he had the right to consult with an attorney. Should this impact your view? Does it telegraph that he is being "oppressed"? Did the officers threaten him when he asked?
- Have you had experience with police that led you not to trust anyone in law enforcement?
- Are you, or are you related to, a law enforcement officer?
- Does that impact your vision?

- Did speech patterns of the law enforcement officers or the suspect impact your thinking?

■ ■ ■ ■ ■

This is just a small list of filters to consider. You know your own filters, so consider them in your analysis. Do you have a vested interest of any kind to have the answer be one or the other? Do you have any bias that affects your data collection and evaluation?

If you have stripped all of those let's move to make a decision.

Decide

We are not going to give you an answer, but we will address some elements as you decide. You may want to augment your knowledge of things you hadn't thought of prior to this. You may also come to appreciate your pre-existing knowledge much more since it is part of what makes you unique in your body-language expertise.

The stage is a functional area for moving the prisoner without public scrutiny at a time when the security of a police station was iconic. This would certainly have an impact on the officers, making them less likely to notice anything familiar. It's like the farmer who doesn't notice the snake in the grass because he always walks that path.

Jack Ruby was a known associate of many police officers. Just more of the scenery.

In blocking, most people are moving as if the environment is unscripted and serving as stimulus. The police officers and people in the room move as if this is "normal" and something they have done a million times. For example, they would hold the suspect to allow media a decent camera angle.

Do you think they were aware they would be on the front page of every newspaper in the United States? Certainly—even before the shooting of Oswald. Does that affect the specific choice of clothing? Yes—even in the more formal hat-wearing 1960s, the two officers nearest to Oswald look particularly dapper for police officers.

Do you think that the photo opportunities impacted openness to allow the photographer to get better images? Remember: This isn't the age of modern media and having your photo in the newspaper was a major event, much less every newspaper in the United States and many outside the country.

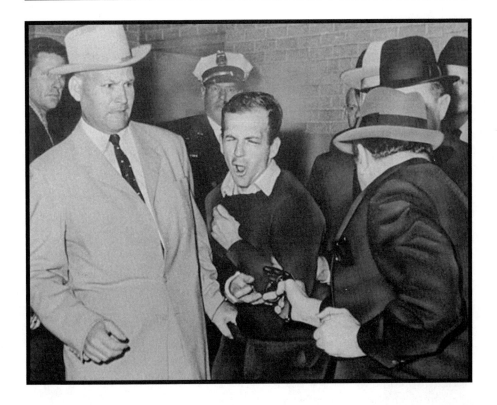

Watch the cadence of the people moving about in a "normal" way. Who looks out of place, rushed, and nervous? After the shooting, does that change?

Now look at their body language immediately before during and after the shooting. There is a transition from fluid-moving and proud posture to rigid, arbitrary movement and grasping. Look further at the facial expressions and signaling. What do you see in each individual? Remembering to strip away your modern-justice sensibility as a filter, and any preconceived notions you had about the case, what does that shift mean?

You saw what looked like a person being handed over to a vigilante in the first image. But now? After analyzing the pieces and parts, is the image the same?

We're getting close to decision time.

Did you see people hand Oswald over to be murdered? Or did you see men who were unsuspecting because they were blinded by a location they have always—iconically—identified as safe? Did you see non-verbal signals of disgust and staged planning, or simply men doing a job who were interrupted by a vigilante? Look at this over and over again. Apply the knowledge you have about the times, the facts of the case, the culture, and the players.

What is your answer: evidence of a conspiracy to kill Oswald, or the act of a vigilante?

Finally, does this image change your impression? Taken at the moment of impact, it shows more detail about the reaction of Oswald's escorts. What do you see and think now?

Which of Ekman's 7 Absolutes is the gentleman in white, homicide detective James Robert Leavelle (left of Oswald in the photo), showing? What about the uniformed officer in the rear? And the man behind the white suit? Does this change anything? If so, why? What do you see differently as a result of this image—even though you watched it unfold "live" on film?

Give yourself permission to do this to other famous cases, celebrities, politicians, and any place you can find video and stills and review over and over again. It is especially effective if you know the outcome like the O.J. Simpson trial or any other big murder trials. What works for these large high-profile cases works locally, too.

Enjoy the process this R.E.A.D. exercise can teach you. It can help to refine the skills you picked up in this book. Take time to Review and catalog signals, Evaluate what is "normal" and what isn't, Analyze the data and strip away your filters, and then Decide what it all means.

Glossary

Active observation: An interrogation term referring to activity that follows *passive observation*; it involves asking questions of people around the source, such as fellow prisoners and prison guards.

Adaptational mirroring: Mirroring done unintentionally; a survival tool. (See Mirroring.)

Adaptors: Gestures to release stress, and to adjust the body as a way to increase the comfort level.

Artifact thinker: Sees discrete package of information in every concept or conversation (see also Icon thinker); a term coined by Gregory Hartley.

Barriers: Postures and gestures we use when we are uncomfortable.

Big 5, The: A term coined by Gregory Hartley to refer to five major categories of movements: gestures, illustrators, regulators, adaptors, and barriers.

Complementary behavior: Mirroring behavior that is like-for-like, for example, responding to pleasantness with pleasantness. (See also Noncomplementary behavior.)

Ekman's Absolutes: In this book, it refers to the seven facial expressions of emotion that are shared across humanity. Psychologist Paul Ekman identified them through extensive field research: fear, sadness, happiness, anger, contempt, disgust, and surprise.

Illustrators: Gestures used to punctuate a statement.

Meta-behaviors: A term coined by Gregory Hartley that groups together major factors that influence body language, primarily mirroring and rituals.

Microculture: A subset of culture that may be as small as two people (for example, a married couple) or a large group, such as Texans.

Mirroring: A natural response to another person, but something that can also be done intentionally to put someone at ease, create discomfort, or otherwise manipulate the person's emotions.

Noncomplementary behavior: Behavior that runs counter to the behavior of another, that is, responding to aggression with a calm, soothing demeanor. (See also Complementary behavior.)

Passive observation: An interrogation term that refers to watching your source to collect a range of useful information.

Primary human drivers: The phrase Gregory Hartley uses to refer to food, sex, and sleep.

R.E.A.D. (Review, Evaluate, Analyze, Decide): The system of reading and using body language developed by Gregory Hartley.

Regulators: Gestures used to control another person's speech.

Rituals: Habitual gestures that include such things as formalized bits of ceremony, microcultural norms, and idiosyncrasies.

Stealth-heroes: Super-typical people in an organization who are vitally important, but not as visible as the alpha.

Sub-typical: A person or group of people who fall on the left side of the bell curve in mapping a culture, tribe, or microculture.

Super-typical: A person or group of people who fall on the right side of the bell curve in mapping a culture, tribe, or microculture.

Symbols: Learned gestures that capture particular sentiments.

Notes

Chapter 1

1. Nathan H. Lents, "Other Primates Use of Speech and Vocabulary," *The Human Evolution* (blog), October 21, 2014, *https://thehumanevolutionblog.com/2014/10/21/other-primates-use-speech-and-vocabulary/*

Chapter 2

1. Jeffrey Davis, "A historical linguistic account of sign language among North American Indian groups," from *Multilingualism and Sign Languages: From the Great Plains to Australia*; C. Lucas (ed.), Gallaudet University Press, 2006, Vol. 12, p. 3–35.

2. Stuart Piggott, *Ancient Europe*, Edinburgh: The University Press, 1965, p. 229.

3. Koen Nelissen, Giuseppe Luppino, Wim Vanduffel, Giacomo Rizzolatti, and Guy Orban, "Observing Others: Multiple Action Representation in the Frontal Lobe," *Science*, Vol. 310, Issue 5746 (2005): 332–336; DOI: 10.1126/science.1115593.

4. Vilayanur Ramachandran, "The neurons that shaped civilization," TEDIndia, November 2009, *www.ted.com/talks/vs_ramachandran_the_neurons_that_shaped_civilization?language=en*

5. Ibid.

6. "Worldwide displacement hits all-time high as war and persecution increase," United Nations High Commission for Refugees, June 10, 2015; *www.unhcr.org/en-us/news/*

latest/2015/6/558193896/worldwide-displacement-hits-all-time-high-war-persecution-increase.html

7. Mark Hugo Lopez, "In 2014, Latinos will surpass whites as largest racial/ethnic group in California," Pew Research Center, *www.pewresearch.org/fact-tank/2014/01/24/in-2014-latinos-will-surpass-whites-as-largest-racialethnic-group-in-california/*

8. Dean Hohl and Maryann Karinch, *Rangers Lead the Way*, Adams Media, 2003, p. 53.

Chapter 3

1. William James, *Principles of Psychology*, pp. 193–195.

2. Kang Lee, "Can you really tell if a kid is lying?," TED2016, February 2016; *www.ted.com/talks/ kang_lee_can_you_really_tell_if_a_kid_is_lying#t-799141*

3. *http://liespotting.com/2010/06/ hillary-clinton%E2%80%99s-diplomatically-deceitful-head-nods/*

4. Cathy Newman, *National Geographic*, September 2006, pp. 74–93.

Chapter 4

1. *ScienceDaily* reporting on the study conducted by the University of Sussex team of Amy Victoria Smith, Leanne Proops, Kate Grounds, Jennifer Wathan and Karen McComb, "Functionally relevant responses to human facial expressions of emotion in the domestic horse (Equus caballus)," *Biology Letters*, February 9, 2016; DOI: 10.1098/rsbl.2015.0907; *www.sciencedaily.com/ releases/2016/02/160209221158.htm*

2. *www.pathintl.org/resources-education/resources/ eaat/60-resources/efpl/201-equine-facilitated-psychotherapy*

3. Kun Guo as quoted by Matthew Stock, "Dogs can read human emotions," February 16, 2016, Reuters; *www.reuters.com/article/ us-dogs-emotions-idUSKCN0VP1DH*

4. William C. Berger, *Doll* (unpublished manuscript, 2016), pp. 279–280.

Chapter 5

1. Claudia Mazzucco, "Lost in Autism, Found by Golf," *Golf Digest*, June 16, 2013, *www.golfdigest.com/story/golf-saved-my-life-claudia-mazzucco*

2. Ibid.

3. Ibid.

4. Claudia Mazzucco (golf history expert and author), in discussion with Maryann Karinch, July 12, 2016.

5. *www.conspiracyclub.co/.*

6. J. Eric Oliver and Thomas J. Wood, "Conspiracy Theories and the Paranoid Style(s) of Mass Opinion," *American Journal of Political Science*, March 5, 2014, DOI: 10.1111/ajps.12084.

7. Susan Scutti, "Brain Facts to Know and Share: Men Have a Lower Percentage of Gray Matter than Women," *Medical Daily*, July 10, 2014, *www.medicaldaily.com/brain-facts-know-and-share-men-have-lower-percentage-gray-matter-women-292530*

8. Ibid.

9. Brigitte Jordan, "Pattern Recognition in Human Evolution and Why It Matters for Ethnography, Anthropology, and Society," *Advancing Ethnography in Corporate Environments*, Left Coast Press, 2013, p. 195.

Chapter 6

1. Marissa Fessenden, "There's a Philly Sign Language Accent," Smithsonian.com, December 4, 2015, *www.smithsonianmag.com/smart-news/theres-philly-sign-language-accent-180957459/?no-ist*

2. Mary Ann Turney and Ruth L. Sitler, "Communication challenges—Gender patterns in talking," *WomanPilot*, July 11, 2011; *http://womanpilot.com/?p=115*

3. Jessica Cassity, "Finger Length Predicts Health and Behavior," *Discover*, May 2013; *http://discovermagazine.com/2013/may/04-finger-length-ratio-can-predict-aggressive-behavior-and-risk-of-disease*

4. Jim McCormick, *The Power of Risk*, Maxwell Press, 2008, pp. 142–143.

5. Louann Brizenden, *The Female Brain*, Random House, 2006, p. 98.

6. Laura S. Allen, Mark F. Richey, Yee M. Chai, and Roger A. Gorski, "Sex Differences in the Corpus Callosum of the Living Human Being," *The Journal of Neuroscience*, April 1991, 11(4): 933–942; *www.jneurosci.org/content/11/4/933.long*

Chapter 8

1. *www.youtube.com/watch?v=LHbg7te2D98*

2. Pam Key, "SE Cupp on Trump's Megyn Kelly Attack: 'Bizarre, Rude Behavior," *The Lead with Jake Tapper*, CNN, August 25, 2015, *www.breitbart.com/video/2015/08/25/se-cupp-on-trumps-megyn-kelly-attack-bizarre-rude-behavior*

3. *www.youtube.com/watch?v=tFgF1JPNR5E*

Index

About the Authors

Gregory Hartley's expertise as a human behavior expert began with a career as a decorated military interrogator and led to business success effecting cultural and transactional transformation for multi-billion-dollar global companies. It has also drawn the intelligence community, Hollywood, and national media to seek his insights regarding body language and behavior.

Hartley's military record includes earning the prestigious Knowlton Award, which recognizes individuals who have contributed significantly to the promotion of Army Intelligence.

Greg is the author of eight books on human behavior.

Maryann Karinch is the author of 25 books, including the best-seller *How to Spot a Liar*, which she coauthored with Gregory Hartley, and the Pulitzer Prize–nominated *The Wandering Mind*, which she coauthored with psychiatrist John Biever.

Earlier in her career, she managed a professional theater and raised funds for arts and education programs in Washington, D.C. She holds bachelor's and master's degrees in speech and drama from The Catholic University of America in Washington, D.C.